The
Enabler

*when helping hurts
the ones you love*

ANGELYN MILLER, MA

The Enabler: When Helping Hurts the Ones You Love

First U.S. edition published in 1988 by Hunter House Inc., Publishers

Second U.S. edition published in 1990 by Ballantine Books

Cover design: Susan Wenger

Published by Wheatmark®
610 East Delano Street, Suite 104
Tucson, Arizona 85705 U.S.A.
www.wheatmark.com

ISBN-13: 978-1-58736-905-6 (hardcover)
ISBN-10: 1-58736-905-2 (hardcover)
ISBN-13: 978-1-58736-067-1 (paperback)
ISBN-10: 1-58736-067-5 (paperback)

LCCN: 2001118474

To the members of my family, who have grown and developed into remarkable people in spite of me.

"The greatest thing in the world is to know how to be self-sufficient."

Michel Eyquem De Montiaigne

CONTENTS

When not in check,
I will:
   pick up your shoes
     carry your pack
       pay your traffic ticket
         lie to your boss
           do your homework
             remove rocks from your path
  and strip you of the joy
    of saying "I did it myself!"

PREFACE TO THE THIRD EDITION

It has been almost twenty years since I first wrote *The Enabler*, and I have had time to look back and reexamine the events that led to the writing of my story.

The story is of a wife and mother struggling with problems stemming from a family dynamic of co-dependency, and of the events which ripped this co-dependency apart. As in earlier editions, the narration of events has been reframed to illustrate the essential concepts of enabling relationships. The names and many details of time and place have been altered.

Since writing *The Enabler*, many things in my life have changed. My children are now all adults, some with children of their own. And shortly after the original publication of this book, I returned to the university to obtain a master's degree in counseling psychology.

I am now able to look at my earlier experiences with the detachment that comes with the passage of time, and a professional point of view. However when one's own life is the subject one can never be totally detached or totally professional.

Simply writing *The Enabler* shifted the course of my life, not dramatically, but measurably. The subsequent years and training continue to bring additional insights, and a regrouping of my thoughts. However, my experience and the events that took place at the time I wrote my story remain the core of *The Enabler*.

ACKNOWLEDGEMENTS

I wish to thank the staff at Wheatmark for helping produce this issue of *The Enabler*. I am also grateful to Kiran Rana of Hunter House, Inc., for his confidence in publishing the initial edition in 1988, and to Sherrill Woodruff, editor, of Ballantine Books for finding the book worthy and useful enough to publish it in a mass-market edition in 1990.

LOOKING FOR THE ANSWER

During the difficult years of my enabling, I knew that something was wrong. Life had not become what I had believed it would. As I watched my husband and children falter in life, one after another, I viewed the situation first with disbelief and then with panic.

When I married Stan in 1958, I wasn't worried about the future of my relationship with him. I had a degree in human development and family relations from a major university. When I had children—Tom, John, Nina, and Bud—I wasn't concerned about what would be required of me as a mother, because I was a credentialed elementary school teacher and knew about children. I should have been ready to be the ideal wife and mother. Indeed, I thought I would be. But my family life evolved through the years in a way for which nothing I had learned prepared me. I moved into a life that was so different from my plans and my imaginings that it took me many years to sort it all out.

The most positive thing I can say about myself during that period is that I did recognize that something was wrong. And, as was typical of our family, it was I who made an effort to understand and find help.

I tried everything. I went to counseling, enrolled in EST training, attended Gestalt workshops, joined encounter groups and women's support groups, and took assertiveness

training and courses in transactional analysis and neurolin-
guistic programming. I provided myself with an incredible
amount of information about personal growth and family
dynamics.

But however well armed with ideas I was, it took a
series of tragic events to turn this theoretical knowledge
into genuine understanding. This is the story of those events.
I have written it in response to the frustration I felt at not
readily finding an explanation for why our family was functioning poorly.

The myriad theories and techniques, which were often
contradictory, only made the picture more obscure. I
wanted to see us accurately, to understand what was hap-
pening to us. I wanted a coherent interpretation, a focused
picture.

Because I thought I was so well trained to be a home-
maker, and because I came from a generation of women
whose principal goal in life was to produce successful
families, I was stunned by the difficulties my family was
experiencing. I attributed them mostly to my husband,
and then to my children, as they grew older. It had never
occurred to me that I could be a major contributor to our
problems.

When a counselor finally pointed me toward Janet
Geringer Woititz's writings on co-dependence and adult
children of alcoholics, I began to understand the dynamics
of our family life and my role in it. The concept of "enabling"
provided the insight I had been searching for. Later still,
after I had worked through my own stages of understanding
and devised a personal therapy, I came across the Twelve
Steps of Alcoholics Anonymous and the complementary
steps of Al-Anon. In essence, my process had been similar
to the one suggested in the Twelve Steps.

My father was an alcoholic, and I was determined to
marry a man who would never abuse alcohol. So I married

a man who was also raised in an alcoholic's household and abhorred alcoholism. While my husband did not drink, he did suffer from recurring bouts of anxiety and depression.

After I married Stan, I thought his first episode of depression and anxiety was simply the result of transitory circumstances. I was sure that if I were cheerful enough, helpful enough, accommodating enough, I could make him feel happy and secure—or I could alter the situation so that he would be happy. His periods of depression were episodic in the same fashion as my father's periodic drinking. My pattern of co-dependency was identical to that of the wife of an alcoholic. When my father went on a binge, my mother scurried around making everything right. I did the same with Stan's depression. I had moved into a relationship very similar to the classic enabler-alcoholic type.

When I finally recognized myself to be an enabling wife, I began to see that my enabling was not limited to my marriage; it permeated my other relationships as well. I was an enabler to other family members, friends, and especially to my children.

I also discovered that the problem of enabling is much more common than I had supposed, and is not limited to cases of substance abuse. There are a great number of people like myself whose principal way of relating to others is to assume their responsibilities.

⁂

Organizations like Al-Anon, and Adult Children of Alcoholics (ACA) have created excellent programs for co-dependents (enablers) of alcoholics and other substance abusers. Their programs, however, overlook the large number of co-dependents of non-alcoholics who could profit from their techniques. While these support organizations don't particularly exclude other types of co-dependents, enablers do not ordinarily think to look their direction.

In my search for useful information that would allow me to understand the dynamics of my family, apart from materials on adult children of alcoholics, I found very little. There seemed a gap in the literature on enabler-dependent relationships of our sort. This book is meant to help fill that gap.

2

PORTRAIT OF AN ENABLER

I was coughing and wheezing from the dust that was hanging in the air, but I had to finish cleaning the basement. The new owners were to move in the next day. The room was a moldy, musty mess, filled with an assortment of junk. There couldn't have been anything there worth more than a dollar or two. I felt like sweeping the whole lot out the door and setting a match to it.

I was so tired from these two weeks of moving that it seemed to take twice the normal effort just to keep my arms in motion. I picked up a mildewed schoolbook that had belonged to my son Tom, a very responsible eighteen-year-old who would be going to college in the fall. I threw it in the pile going to the dump.

My youngest son, Bud, who had just turned thirteen, was hefting boxes up the stairs and carting them across the backyard to John, who was loading the truck. John, just sixteen, was the huskiest of the three.

As Tom helped me move everything off the dirt floor and onto the slab of concrete by the entry, I saw that our belongings had multiplied far out of proportion to our years of living in this house. A good half of them didn't seem worthy of the move, but I continued to sort, throwing most things into the pile whose fate was questionable.

I was pleased that my sons had come with me to help.

It wasn't voluntary, though. Their father had insisted. Nina, fifteen and our only daughter, evaded the command by promising to stay home to unpack dishes and put the kitchen in order.

Most of the heavy items had been loaded when a couple of Bud's friends came by to ask if he could go with them to a softball game. I hated to take up his whole weekend, so I let him go, and John went with him. Tom and I were left to finish up the job.

It wasn't too long before I heard rumblings coming from Tom's direction. He dumped what was left of Stan's tools into a big box and asked angrily, "Why isn't Dad over here helping us?"

I had asked Stan earlier if he would go over to the old house to clean the basement so that I could stay home to unpack boxes. I had to be back at my job on Monday. It would take a lot of time to organize a household for six people, and once my work began again, I would only have the evenings to complete the task. I was already disappointed that I had used up my annual vacation on the move without finding time to do any relaxing.

Stan had refused to help clean the basement. He said, "You know how much I hate moving and how terrible I'll feel if I go back and see that house again." I understood. Moving made Stan depressed. He had a hard time letting go of things, especially houses. His contribution this day had been to wake the boys early and make them come with me.

All I could say to Tom was, "You know how your dad hates to move. He was afraid he would get depressed if he came back to this house." Tom got quiet and continued to work. But the cellar was dark, depressing, and dirty—and Tom looked so miserable that I finally said, "I'm mostly finished. Why don't you carry out what's left and drive the truck to the new place? I'll finish up and come over in the car."

It hadn't looked like three hours of work, but it was four o'clock when I pulled into the driveway of our new house. No one was home. There was a note on the refrigerator letting me know that Stan, Nina and Tom had gone bicycling. The dishes hadn't been unpacked.

I rummaged around for a pot to boil some water to make myself a cup of coffee, hoping for one more burst of energy before the day was over. I was angry that they had the leisure to play while I did not. Yet I had been the one who had let them off the hook.

I ignored my anger because I knew that once they walked back through the door my resentment would disappear. I loved them.

In many ways, we were an unusual family. We did not appear to be much different from other families, especially when the children were small, but as they matured, more problems arose with each of us than our family circumstances appeared to justify. It was a matter of the unit being more "regular" than its parts. Our children functioned very well within the family structure, but found coping with the outside world inexplicably difficult.

We were close, caring, and supportive of one another in emotional moments and trials and we did many activities together. These qualities caused other young people to try to adopt us as their family. We were exceptionally tolerant of each other's individual quirks; we allowed and respected differences. It was perhaps this tolerance that attracted others to us, and ironically it was this very tolerance that ultimately caused problems.

I began unpacking cups and saucers and placing them in the cupboard. I knew why I hadn't asked Stan to do more than the loading and unloading of the furniture. I was trying to prevent him from going into a depression over the move. For a good portion of our marriage, he had had spells of depression and anxiety. I did what I could to prevent them or mitigate them. I was doing so now. I was allowing him to "play" to soften his suffering. I was glad, too, that Nina had gone with her father bicycling. It was worth putting the dishes away to give her this opportunity to be with her father. She so often felt ignored by him, especially when he was depressed. She, too, occasionally felt anxiety and mild depression. I was worried about her.

It was my son John, however, who gave me the most concern. He didn't seem to fit well in any context but his home. Most of the time he was a loving, well-behaved, cheerful young man, but at other times his behavior was nothing short of outrageous. I reassured myself by believing that he was a highly intelligent, sensitive, creative person who shouldn't have his uniqueness stifled.

They were special people, these children and this husband of mine. I did what I could to smooth the rough spots in their lives. Why? Because I was an enabler. I unconsciously supported their eccentricity. I now admit this with both distress and embarrassment. It is a crushing admission.

3

PORTRAIT OF A DEPENDENT

I met Stan when I was sixteen years old and I knew that one day I would marry him. It wasn't a pressing thing; it was just a conviction I had.

Stan combined all of the traits that I wanted in a husband. He was kind, intelligent, full of humor and had a special quality, which I call "nobility." Most important, he was not like my father.

We had a very strong sense of camaraderie and sharing from the beginning. Also he, like me, came from an alcoholic family. His home life had been different from mine in that his mother was not an emotionally strong woman. Mine was. When his father was drinking, their household fell apart. As a result, Stan suffered the effects of alcoholism more intensely than I did—or so I thought at the time. But, in fact, while he was learning to be anxious and depressed, I was learning to enable.

Stan and I played at romance for about seven years before we finally married. Having both come from homes that were much less than ideal, we did not see marriage as glamorous, so we felt no rush. We did vow, however, that our family would never be like those of our childhoods.

An incident that happened before we were married foretold the trouble we would later have, but I was too naïve to recognize it. Problems that happen prior to a marriage are often viewed as somehow not real, or as difficulties that will be solved by the marriage (marriage regularly being viewed as a cure-all for a multitude of problems).

We were in our sophomore year at college, attending universities that were fifty miles apart. The separation bothered Stan. He became distraught and came to see me often for comfort and support. In one way, his need was inhibiting, but in another way I loved it. I loved feeling that I was a support for someone, that I was useful, that I was needed.

I spent hours talking him through what had come to be his main concern—what he wanted to do with his life. We discussed this endlessly. What he said he wanted was vague and not specific enough for me. He talked philosophically, while I spoke in practical terms. I was a good listener, and he seemed such a worthy person. I would have done anything to help him.

Stan transferred from his school to mine, and we continued probing his inner feelings in his search for himself. He was nervous and confused, and I felt strong and capable of helping.

Even before we married, I was worried about what our relationship had become, but I was young and thought perhaps we were just going through the normal course of a deepening relationship. I couldn't look to my parents for guidance because they didn't have the kind of marriage I wanted. Stan's parents were so troubled that they had always been useless to him as counselors, and I may have been the first person in his life that he could really talk to.

There were others I could have married, but besides Stan having all of the qualities I valued, I thought Stan needed me. I believed that I was the one person who understood him, loved him, appreciated him, and could help him become whatever he chose to become. I knew when I married him that I was taking on a project. But he was so bright and so talented that I expected, with me by his side, that there would be no end to what he could achieve.

I assumed my rewards would come through my husband's accomplishments. Personal fulfillment for a family-oriented woman was having a comfortable house in a friendly neighborhood with a husband who was successful and children who were at the head of their class. I had been taught this, I believed it, and it felt right. So Stan and I had a common goal—to help him become what he wanted to be. We focused on him. His success would bring family success.

Stan seemed to have been born with a mid-life crisis. He was never sure that he was doing what he was meant to do in life, but as long as he worked hard and kept busy he functioned well and felt good.

We started the uphill battle of developing an adult life. I began having babies at a rapid rate, and Stan held down a job and continued graduate school. We created so many responsibilities for ourselves that we no longer thought about which way the stream was flowing. We just allowed ourselves to be carried along by the current.

As we moved through those early years of struggle, Stan did well. I didn't. Being tied down with four small children was isolating me more and more. I had developed an image of myself as perpetually pregnant and plump. Simply taking my children to the supermarket was overwhelming. Going on a family picnic had become a burden. I was gradually becoming a recluse, beginning to feel unsure of myself in social situations. During this period while Stan was climbing the career ladder, he seemed to never be home, and I rarely left the house. When he was home, he seemed distracted and ill at ease. He would sporadically initiate projects with the children, but was inconsistent because it seemed he couldn't bear not to be working. I thought his discomfort from being at loose ends meant that he preferred not being with me and the children. I felt that the world was passing me by and taking my husband along.

Our roles had changed. I had become desperately in need of his attention and time, and he was busy. I had become his burden. The game was the same, but we had switched positions.

Then something with the impact of an emotional earthquake happened, shifting the structure again. Stan completed graduate school. It should have brought him relief and rejoicing, but instead, it brought a job decision—which translated into a life decision—and Stan faltered.

Up to this point, Stan had been able to put off making any career decisions while working to finish his degree. When he was offered a lucrative post on the West Coast, that he was not sure he wanted to take, he was paralyzed. He had been carrying submerged feelings of confusion from being raised in a confused household. These feelings surfaced again.

Stan had spent his childhood with unstable parents moving from one place to another, and he had grown to fear any household move. This opportunity, to which he was so drawn, required moving to an area of the country that was new to us. He now had to make a decision between his present job, which wouldn't require a move, and the new offer, which he wanted. Neither option, however, offered the opportunity to contribute to society in the grandiose manner that he had envisioned, and he was sucked back into his "meaning of life" trauma.

Stan spent sleepless nights pacing the floor, talking to me incessantly about the question of moving. He dredged up all of his old fears and worries about his desire to do something significant. It became once more the consuming preoccupation of us both.

Stan became obsessed with his dilemma and was becoming increasingly dysfunctional. He made the decision repeatedly to accept the new appointment. He had to make it repeatedly, because he was unable to follow through with it.

His friends began avoiding him because his only topic of conversation was his anxiety over trying to make a career decision. He would also seek out people to ask their advice. I shared this obsession and allowed it to become mine.

Because I was so preoccupied with Stan, I began to neglect the emotional needs of the children. All the daily problems and natural happenings in the family became secondary. As his anxiety grew, I took on the task of manipulating our environment so that he would be relieved of any unnecessary emotional distress.

It is said, "trouble never leaves you where it finds you." While Stan was going through one of the most devastating periods of his life, I was going through a metamorphosis. As friends and acquaintances were changing their opinions of Stan, they were also changing their opinion of me. I was being praised for my strength, courage, calmness, patience, understanding, selflessness, competence, and wisdom. I had become a heroine! And I was needed and loved by my husband! How's that for snatching victory out of the jaws of defeat?

Circumstances forced a decision, and we moved to the West Coast. There we sought medical help for Stan's anxiety. We learned that his prolonged unresolved situation had triggered a major episode of clinical depression. Gradually, he recovered his equilibrium and our life began to normalize, but the trauma had altered us both. He was demoralized and insecure about his abilities, and lived continuously on the verge of depression. I, although living in fear that I couldn't forever keep juggling the needs and demands of Stan, the children, and the wolf at the door, was gathering strength.

A shift in the family dynamic had occurred. Life had

returned to the way it had been in the early part of our marriage. I was in control, and it was an easy role for me, a natural role—the role that my mother had filled.

The years that followed continued to be somewhat troubled. Stan was in and out of depression, and I was again in the position of trying to make a troubled man happy.

I worked hard at trying to pull Stan out of his periodic episodes of depression, but I came to realize that my efforts always seemed to produce the opposite effect to what I had intended. The more cheerful I acted, the more morose he became. When I offered a positive solution, he would tell me that the only reason I could have made such a foolish suggestion was because I didn't fully understand the situation.

Stan didn't want to be consoled; he wanted me to participate in his sadness. He needed me not only to keep his physical environment intact, but also to support his emotional drama. Stan was clearly becoming my emotional dependent.

4

DEPENDENCY

The basic give and take that grants survival and makes people feel secure is not what I mean when I refer to the type of dependence supported by enablers. There is a difference between healthy interdependence and parasitic dependence, but that crucial difference is hard to see in the flurry of family life.

Interdependence is an indispensable pillar of human life. It is a natural and purposeful component of survival, and is the foundation of stable family structure. All people are compelled to rely on others at various times and to varying degrees. They need adult nurturing and protection while growing up. And as adults, they take care of their family members who are old or ill and can't care for themselves. People gain a feeling of security in knowing that their families and friends will take care of them when they are in need. People know what group membership entails, and they know this from growing up in families and communities. They also participate in the interdependence of a broader society. They are aware that most of us would starve if truckers didn't transport food from the farms to the markets. Our society prides itself on maintaining a balance that allows individuals their personal independence within an environment of cultural interdependence. As individuals, people are expected not only to care for themselves but also to contribute to their families, communities and country.

Even people who are chronically ill or disabled and have perfectly justifiable reasons for being dependent are still expected, like everyone else, to do whatever they are able. And those who take their handicaps as a challenge and excel inspire awe, and society makes heroes of them.

Helping others through temporary emotional distress is also part of our ethic. People do get sick, die, have accidents, and experience any number of tragedies. These vicissitudes are part of life, and people recognize it is likely that some disaster will happen to them at one time or another. Grief over tragic events or any kind of devastating loss is normal. Still, after an appropriate length of time, whatever the tragedy, people are expected to face their situation and move on with their personal and professional lives.

It is the differences in the way individuals respond to hard times that separate those who are simply sharing in an interdependent society from those who are dependent.

People who use their disability, grief or adversity as an excuse to avoid doing what they can are emotionally dependent, and emotional dependence can be even more deadly than economic dependence.

Emotional dependents will grasp past or present, real or imagined disappointments as a justification for inaction or pseudo-action. They lay claim to some unwinnable battle and then assert that they could go out into the world and slay dragons, if it weren't for everything that is conspiring against them. As in shadow boxing, their jabs can't connect with anything real or solid. Some people's entire lives revolve around external overwhelming and irresolvable problems. They are always involved in some crisis that they can't or are unwilling to resolve. When these people with "irresolvable problems" turn them over to others to handle, and there are willing takers, the cycle of enabling-dependence begins.

Dependents may show a great deal of energy thrashing about for solutions, but because they are afraid of decision, resolution and action, there is no real drive toward an actual way out. Dependents usually create unique explanations for not finding answers to their problems, but what really lies beneath their reasoning is fear of change, or failure—or fear of losing their enabler.

When friends or family members offer practical answers to a confirmed dependent, their suggestions will be met with every conceivable objection. When enablers scurry around trying to make things OK by "looking at the positive side" and offering real solutions, they are often ridiculed by their dependents for being naïve "Pollyannas" who simply don't appreciate the intractability of the problem.

It took a number of years for me to come to the realization that being a Pollyanna is a preferable way to react to difficulties. It slowly dawned on me that needing to have something wrong in order to justify one's behavior is inherently a negative cycle. If, as Idealist philosophers assert, life is what one perceives it to be, why not perceive it to be bountiful and benevolent? An optimistic attitude can help to produce happiness. If "what you see is what you get," it makes eminently more sense to see good than bad. At a practical level, this philosophy is very simple. Those who see living as a rewarding experience are able to have more pleasant lives. Those who insist on viewing living as painful and difficult will find pain and difficulty in everything.

I spent hours with Stan trying to help him work out a plan of action that would allow him to step out of his circular obsession and move forward. I was looking for results; he was avoiding results.

Stan felt victimized by an unfair world that would not

offer him the exact job he wanted in the precise location he chose. To him, there was no solution to this problem. Although he finally had to compromise, in his heart there was no compromise. I erroneously believed during this time of decision trauma that Stan wanted to make a decision and that he wanted me to help. In hindsight, I see that all of his flailing about was done to protect him from having to make a decision. What he wanted from me was not help to find some practical answer but someone to participate in his trauma and grief over an imperfect life.

Struggling for independence in a competitive world is difficult for everyone, but it is especially hard for children who have had an inadequate parental model.

Stan told me that when his father was drinking, his parents would become so engrossed in their own drama that they ignored him. It was only when he would indicate signs of sadness or distress about the drinking that they would pay attention to him. As a child, Stan was genuinely anxious, but it's sad that his only way of getting them to notice him was to be more distraught than they were. It is easy to see how, under these circumstances, a person could grow up believing that life is a continuing ordeal and that the one way to be acknowledged is to be unhappy and anxious.

Children from homes where upheaval is a regular part of life can easily carry, for the rest of their lives, the fear that catastrophe is around every corner. Or worse, they imprint on their parents' lifestyle and don't know how to operate in any other climate. These children, watching other people leading what looks like happy normal lives, feel like victims who have been cheated out of some essential ingredient that is required for living. They often develop a sense of shame or unworthiness, while at the same time holding an unrealistic image of how other people live. This confusion and uncertainty about how to live life continues with them into adulthood.

People learn very early in life which behaviors earn them the strokes they need. If they are unable to get the strokes they want, they settle for those they can get, and they use whatever tactic it takes to get them. As they pass through adult years, they carry their early childhood patterns of behavior with them, reforming as they go according to the rewards and punishments they are receiving. While many people jump fearlessly into the adult world, dependents are reluctant and check first to see if they really want to participate. If the adult world appears too frightening, they can develop non-participating strategies for self-protection.

Dependents will use their traumas to keep others tied to them, making it hard for giving, feeling people to abandon them. It is very difficult for an enabler to break this spell. On some level dependents know this, and they are able to keep their spouses, parents, children, or friends tied to them indefinitely. A sick man who feels that his wife will leave him may move from one illness to another to keep her, unconsciously unaware of what he is doing. He only knows that he feels ill and can't survive without her, and he makes sure that she knows that he desperately needs her.

Becoming stuck in their misery seemingly without having the ability to move on, dependents' pain seems so genuine and their situation so unbearable that others are easily pulled into their problems. Instinctively, compulsive enablers will stick with them, only helping to perpetuate the drama.

Friends will listen, offer suggestions, and do what they can to help—until they realize that the dependent is not seeking a solution, only commiseration. At that point, the friends move on and away, and the dependent looks for new friends.

Dependents pay a serious price for their unwillingness to face the world on the world's terms. Abdicating their affairs to spouses, friends, bosses or whomever costs them control. Many decisions made on their behalf may not turn out to be what the dependents would have chosen, had they been thinking clearly and independently.

While enablers are rather drab characters, being practical rule-followers and hard workers, their dependents are often romantic figures, perpetually preoccupied with their own dramas.

To me, my husband was a magnificent, stricken eagle, and by comparison, I felt like a domestic duck. Being reliable and predictable can be a bore to others.

Stan often said, "I hate the word adjust. It is like someone going into my head with a wrench and tightening screws or loosening bolts. Why should I adjust?" I never had an answer. Somehow, his indignation over this seemed justified. The world should have been more accommodating. I was.

Not having an answer for the question "Why should I adjust?" kept me in my place. It was in one of those a-ha flashes that the answer came to me: No one has to adjust! But there is a price to be paid for not doing so. Stan was paying the price, but was borrowing the money from me.

People have the right to behave as they wish, but every type of behavior has a corresponding consequence. There are natural laws governing human interaction. Social customs have generally evolved for the good of all. These principles, with their system of rewards and punishments, form the ecology of your emotional world. You can accept or reject established patterns, but you don't have the option of rejecting the consequences. The consequences follow. If you are not willing to endure the results of a particular type of behavior, then you must change that behavior.

The consequence of not adjusting to the reality of your world is being prevented from fully participating in it. Dependent people are non-players. But dependents cannot remain dependents if they have no one to play their parts for them.

5

MY SON JOHN

Shattering the connection of enabler-dependent relationships is the ultimate threat to both the dependent and the
enabler. Over the years, they have developed and cultivated
a very deeply rooted way of relating to each other and to
other people. Any change in this pattern threatens the very
idea of who they are, whether the change is forced by circumstances or initiated to achieve health.

I had lived through many an earthquake with Stan's
bouts of anxiety and depression, and I was still standing—
just tall enough to be struck by lightning. Being struck by
lightning is the most apt metaphor I know to express how
a family feels when one of its members is stricken with a
serious brain disorder.

It began in the summer before John's twentieth birthday.
He suddenly became extremely agitated. He believed that
one of his friends had slipped a drug, perhaps angel dust,
into his drink.

John became so paranoid that he was unable to sleep in
his own bedroom. He believed that the same friend entered
the house at night and injected him with a damaging drug
while he slept. After the family retired, he would go into a
bathroom that had no windows, lock the door, and try to
sleep on the floor. He felt so vulnerable when asleep that he
was soon almost never sleeping. His growing fatigue began

making it hard for him to go to his summer job, and when he went, it was difficult for him to remain the entire day. As his conviction that he had been poisoned grew into an obsession, he started working out with weights to increase his strength in case he needed to protect himself.

Watching him pace back and forth in the living room almost at a run was frightening. I didn't know what to believe or how to react. It was not beyond the realm of possibility that there had been a very cruel trick played on him, triggering a chemical imbalance in his brain. Whatever precipitated John's frenzied disorientation, it was the most severe tragedy I could have imagined.

We had taken John to a physician two months previously for an extraordinarily severe headache. He was hospitalized for a day, given medication for pain, and told that he had a cluster headache that would eventually go away. It did. When he first became agitated and claimed that he had been poisoned, we took him to a psychiatrist. Having dealt with drug-related psychosis, the doctor believed there might well be a possibility that John's distress and paranoia were the result of a toxic substance. A blood test didn't indicate there was anything unusual in his system, however, so there was nothing we could do but wait and observe his behavior.

Then John called us one day from a pay phone near his job and said, "Come get me, I've been wandering around." We called a psychiatrist, who made arrangements for him to be admitted to a hospital. When we picked John up, we didn't bring him home. We drove one hundred miles to the nearest psychiatric hospital that had an opening.

After leaving Johnny at the hospital, both Stan and I were stunned. The doctors had indicated that John appeared to have a serious brain disorder. I couldn't stop crying. Stan was quiet and tried to comfort me. But he, too, was heartbroken and beaten. I was good at handling crises, but this was far beyond me. I found it unbelievable that my handsome young boy, with so much promise, could be stricken so disastrously and swiftly.

John was our middle son. He had always been very creative and bright. His early childhood had been filled with active, happy play. After we moved into a country home, his main interest had been raising animals for Four-H projects, and through that experience he had developed a sensitive, accepting, and warm nature.

He was always so kind-hearted, fun loving and creative that I didn't allow myself to see any out-of-the-ordinary traits he may have had. I missed the telltale signs that should have warned me of possible trouble ahead. I had always believed that people come in a variety of packages, and have known that some of the great contributors to society have been different. When I did notice something unusual in his behavior, I always passed it off as part of being creatively unique.

As Johnny was growing up, my interaction with him was similar to my interaction with my husband. I allowed him his eccentricities, covered for him, did his household chores, and anticipated his needs. I had rationalized his dropping out of school during his senior year, and welcomed him home without question when he failed to complete basic training in the army.

While I had been willing to overlook John's occasionally aberrant behavior, others had not. He had an insatiable craving for attention. Stan spent countless hours with John, helping with various animal projects. When Stan was in one of his depressions, however, he became less aware of his immediate surroundings, including his children. Johnny's siblings accepted the situation and simply involved themselves in projects that didn't include their dad. But it was always important to John to have contact with his father, and he would follow Stan around, talking incessantly, trying to get a response. Sometimes this was annoying to Stan, but most of the time he was barely aware that John was even there.

Johnny's need for attention was also evident in his school and social life. His hyperactivity and clownish behavior in the third grade had prompted the teacher to suggest that he be medicated with Ritalin to calm him. I became angry and felt that the teacher only wanted him drugged so she wouldn't have to deal with his creativity. Despite his lack of focus, John easily maintained an average school performance. Had I not been an enabling mother, I might have been able to recognize that he suffered from a hyperactivity disorder and might have sought help for him. His outbursts of outlandish behavior continued until, as a teenager, he would do or say outrageous things merely for shock value.

I chided him when he did something absurd, and the word chide is so right for what I did. My chiding was an ineffectual admonition that implied that his behavior could be continued without any serious consequence.

It wasn't until the summer after John came home from the hospital that an incident occurred which forced me to look at myself and see some of my responsibility for his unacceptable behavior.

A group of family and friends was gathered in our living room. John began making outrageous comments designed to embarrass his sister and me. When I mentioned the incident later to my youngest son, Bud, he told me in a burst of anger that it was my fault that John didn't know how to act. He said I had allowed him to be the way he was because I either pretended I didn't hear or called it "a phase," and I had never said, "Stop it!"

I decided to see if Bud was right. I talked to John and told him that his comments during that incident had been completely unacceptable to me and that I would not allow him to speak that way in my house again. John was stunned and quiet because he was so completely shocked by my reaction. It was so out of character. I don't know how he felt internally, but I do know that sort of incident did not happen again. In spite of his illness, he understood and accepted limits.

During those years in which I thought I was such a kind, tolerant, loving mother, I had enabled him to develop a pattern of behavior that was unacceptable to those outside his family. John had so many endearing qualities that it had been too easy for me to overlook and forgive his unusual behavior. He was very loved and had been tolerated by the whole family.

John has since been diagnosed as having a schizoaffective disorder. I can see now that the seed of the illness was within him, and was the result of factors far beyond my control. While I didn't cause the illness, I did support it, in the same way that I fed my husband's depression. I had tried to protect them from the demands of their environment. What they needed was to learn to face their problems and accommodate their illnesses to the realities and demands of the world.

I lived through Stan and John's traumas, and made them my own. There were many times during the years of juggling the whole mess that I thanked God that I had been there for them and had been strong enough to handle the burden. I didn't know that God would have likely replied: "Would you get out of the way, so these people can learn to help themselves?"

6

THE TURNING POINT

During those dark days, I rushed around trying to do what I could to maintain the stability of my family. I didn't know what to do to help Johnny, who was still in the hospital, and I didn't know how to handle the effect his illness had on each member of the family. The situation was too serious to allow myself to blunder through it, and I no longer trusted my own judgment.

My personal search intensified. I reviewed every self-help program available to me. While I felt that they all offered me some new bit of understanding, it was the interplay of seemingly unrelated family events that brought me the insight I needed to change my way of relating to others.

My son's illness had done several things to me. Most important, it put everything else into perspective. All other problems seemed like minor irritations by comparison. Even my husband's bouts with anxiety and depression seemed inconsequential. In the past, helping Stan through one of those periods had been the principal struggle of my life. I now found myself catapulted into a different state of mind. Only Johnny's agony (and he was going through so much of it) and my own grief were important to me. But John was in the hospital and there was nothing I could do at the time but return to the routine things that make up day-to-day living.

I began by turning my attention to the yard work and house repair which had been postponed. I called a tree specialist to spray our trees for bark beetles. After looking at the trees, the tree surgeon suggested we cut down a particularly large pine in the front yard that was still quite beautiful but badly infested. I knew we needed firewood, so without much thought I had Bud and one of his friends cut it down for me.

When Stan came home from work and saw the felled tree, he completely came apart. He was very angry with me. He hadn't wanted the tree cut. Despite the tree surgeon's advice, Stan thought he could have saved it. He began doing what, in the past, had brought me to my knees and to his side—he went into a depression over the loss of the tree. He walked around randomly in a completely distraught state and refused to be comforted. It was a pattern of behavior I had become familiar with and accustomed to since our college days. I had seen him through dozens of such periods.

There was something different this time, however, and the difference was me. I was grieving for my son. Johnny was all I could think about, and I didn't give a damn about that tree. I looked at Stan, and for the first time, instead of looking heartrending to me, he looked foolish. Then I became angry. How dare he mount this big production over a tree when his son was sick in the hospital a hundred miles away? My anger not only kept me from responding sympathetically, but also caused me to lash out at him. I said two things that hit their mark. One was that he was behaving like a spoiled child who hadn't gotten his way. The other was that, while he fancied himself a misunderstood tragic hero, when he was acting like this he appeared to others as simply a nut!

My assertions and my altered attitude, coming on the heels of his own soul-searching about Johnny's condition, produced nothing short of a miracle in Stan. He changed his behavior immediately. I knew that what I had said had been unforgivably cruel, but for the first time in all the years of trying to help him, I actually had.

The tremendous importance of what had just happened didn't sink in immediately because I was still feeling traumatized by what seemed like the loss of my son.

Within the month, a new crisis came into Stan's life. We sold our house. Stan had agreed to sell it earlier because we were a shrinking family in a five-bedroom home. We had enjoyed the house for more than four years, but we now needed the money for our children's college expenses.

Stan went into his moving trauma again. In the past, I had always agreed to anything to accommodate his feelings. If he said, "I don't want to move," I would reply, "You don't have to; we will figure out some way to do whatever you want to do." This time, when he started into the first phase of what I now call unacceptable behavior, I countered it. I told him, "There is no way you're going to get out of this agreement. We need the money and we don't need the house. I will not back out, and I won't allow you to. If you suffer an anxiety attack, I will put you in the hospital and continue the sale, so you may as well shape up and not sabotage the deal."

As a result of my new attitude, Stan worked to help with the sale of the house and was later pleased with himself for having done so.

I had begun changing the way I responded to everyone in the family. I put up with less and demanded more. An awareness of how I was changing didn't dawn on me until an interchange took place that involved John and my mother. My mother, eighty-five at the time, was a fragile but very alert woman. She was spending the month with

us, as she did annually. That year it wasn't particularly con-
venient because Johnny was home from the hospital and
his behavior wasn't always predictable.

One day Johnny started one of his bizarre monologues
and began talking about outrageous things in front of my
mother. That universal disposition, which demands respect
for mothers above all, came over me. I took John aside,
sick as he was, and said, "That is my mother. Don't you
ever, ever, say another outlandish or offensive thing in her
presence." I had always listened to his paranoid ramblings
about other people, trying to be reasonable and talk him
out of his delusions. But this one I would not tolerate, and
he knew it. During the rest of my mother's visit he was
cautious and respectful.

I was again astonished by the revelation that I didn't
have to allow John to do as he pleased just because he was
ill. This may be a simple observation to most people, but to
a consummate enabler it is a powerful insight.

In this instance, my primary concern was my mother.
Johnny was secondary. I did what felt instinctively right to
me, without trying to justify Johnny's behavior or accommodate his illness. Just as my concern for Johnny had interfered
with my giving Stan special attention for his inappropriate behavior, my feelings for my mother had taken priority
over John's illness. Both times I forgot my enabling behavior,
letting whatever might happen as a result, happen.

Instead of trying to manipulate Stan into being happy
and John into being respectful, I let them know that I, personally, had no intention of tolerating the way they were
behaving. The process of returning the burden of their
behavior back to them had begun.

What I had experienced changed forever the way I saw
myself in relation to my family. This fundamental shift in
viewpoint precipitated a remarkable change in the way I
reacted. I no longer felt compelled to be Stan and John's

keeper. By allowing them to take care of their own needs, I was released from an overwhelming job. It was the best gift I could give to the three of us.

7

ASSESSING MYSELF

Things happen to you, but you also happen to them. The knowledge that I had allowed, perhaps supported, both my son's and my husband's behavior struck me with such force that the scrutiny I had given them, I now turned on myself. They had happened to me, but I had also happened to them. I had learned all that I could about their illnesses. It had never occurred to me that I might be fostering those illnesses or that my role in the family dynamics represented a sickness too.

As I mentioned earlier, the concept individual responsibility is central to an interdependent society. Unfortunately, I had focused on the "be responsible for yourself" part and had missed its corollary "and let others be responsible for themselves."

Why had this obvious understanding of human interaction eluded me? Had I imprinted on a particular role model so early in my life that I was incapable of seeing other models? Did my self-esteem hinge on being responsible for others?

It was at this time that a family counselor gave me a book by Janet Geringer Woititz, which he thought would be helpful. At first I was put off by the title, *Marriage on the Rocks*, because "on the rocks" referred to alcohol and neither my husband nor I drink. And I didn't like the implication that my marriage was in trouble.

I suppose things come to people when they are ready for them, because that book reached me in a way that nothing else had. The description of the wife of an alcoholic was me. It was incredible to me that Stan and I, who both hated alcohol and swore we would never have a home like the ones we had come from, were portrayed in the pages of this book. We had the same neurotic patterns, without the chemical substance.

An alcoholic is a person with compulsions and a chemical problem. The spouse of an alcoholic, unless he or she has learned to be different, is usually an enabler. And I was an enabler, even though my husband had never used alcohol or drugs. Enabling is every bit as much a malady as alcoholism, depression, or mania.

I wasn't born an enabler. I learned it by watching how my mother handled her difficult situation. Like many children raised in an alcoholic family, I responded by being a very helpful, obedient, cheerful child. I believed that poor behavior on my part would only be an additional burden on our already stressed family. My father's drinking always unsettled me, but mostly I felt sorry for him and even more sorry for my mother.

In spite of the distress our family continually seemed to be suffering, I bounced through my childhood believing that I was learning what life was all about. I watched how my parents responded to each other and how they raised their children. There were things I didn't like about the way my parents managed their household, and I promised myself that I would not create a home like theirs. I planned to take the good and discard the bad. But I had absorbed their model, unaware that much of my mother's behavior would become my own.

Living on a farm the first few years of my life helped me through the times when things were chaotic—meaning when Daddy was drunk—because I had places to go to avoid being underfoot. Having older brothers and sisters who helped my mother hold things together, I was able to watch at a distance, always telling myself that I would never marry a man like my dad. I worried about my mom, but I knew that she was tough. She was quiet, stoic, and tough. It was difficult not to follow the pattern my parents had set for me. As an adult, I am often jolted by glimpses of myself mimicking my mother. I have unwittingly and unwillingly picked up many of her traits and pattern of interacting.

Examining my childhood now, it is not too difficult to see how I became an enabler. My mother was a self-contained, reliable woman. She was not an affectionate person like my father, but she was consistent and stable. There were times when I knew we were in deep financial trouble and my mother always tried to protect us children from knowing about it. She even protected my father. My father had the luxury of being able to go on his periodic binges because my mother would keep things intact for him. She lived during a difficult era with the huge responsibility of six children. I'm sure she felt that she could not run the risk of leaving my father. She didn't know what disasters might follow if she failed to maintain the household when my father faltered. What she did was for her own survival and for the protection of her children.

Accommodating my father's irresponsibility was a big part of the burden my mother carried. I learned how to be a mother and a wife from her. But my life and circumstances are different from hers. Emulating her stoic patterns in my circumstances has not only been ineffective for me, it has been unhealthy for my family.

Society also nudged me into the role of enabler from the time I was born. Thousands of subtle cues told me that my principal role as a woman was to please. This fit well. I was accustomed to the role of pleaser. Accommodating others had always earned me the strokes I needed and also some measure of control over my circumstances. It was easy to accept this as the right approach and even to become self-righteous about it.

It takes more than pressure from external sources, however, to make people act in a specific way. Behavior has to consistently fill a need. In spite of the image of strength, competence, and control that I often projected, I was insecure. And that insecurity fostered the role I played. I needed to be needed. My self-esteem depended on it. So, unconsciously, and sometimes consciously, I manipulated the circumstances of my life to place myself in a position of being needed.

There are many paths people take to build self-esteem. Most are positive, but some can have an ugly side. Trying to build self-esteem by excelling at something is commendable. When excellence doesn't happen, most people establish themselves in the social and professional hierarchy and comfortably settle in. But there are some who never become comfortable with where they fit best, and strive only to look better than the next guy. It is this "better than the next guy" attitude that can cause trouble. Too often, getting ahead means pushing someone else behind.

It is a rare person who, at some time or other, doesn't have problems with negative self-esteem. It comes with having to accommodate to their social structure. Most enablers can, however, appear so confident and in control that their lack of self-esteem is not apparent.

People who choose partners or friends who are troubled may be doing so only out of their poor sense of self-worth. They are looking for an enabler-dependent relationship to build their self-esteem. Such relationships, though often full of torment, can develop a secure and complementary form of stability. But should enablers actually succeed in helping their dependents, which supposedly was their original goal, their relationship may weaken, causing them both to feel threatened. To maintain the bond, enablers and dependents sometimes unwittingly sabotage progress-enablers by continuing to treat their dependents as fragile and helpless, and dependents by trying to remain that way.

There is a hidden acknowledgment in the enabler's destructive support: A weak partner is better than no partner at all. Thus strong enablers of weak dependents fear that should their dependents actually become successful, they may no longer need or want their enablers. Enablers worry that they may only be wanted because they are needed. Unconsciously, they may be holding on to their dependents by perpetuating their weaknesses.

%%

I had married Stan, a wonderful young man who needed me. But when he became involved in life and began trading problems for successes, my own sense of worth plummeted. I needed to be an enabler to feel worthy of Stan's respect, but he no longer needed an enabler. He was capably working full time to support the children and me. He was completing his graduate studies and earning good money at a research laboratory. He was associated with a musical group that required his time and talent. Stan wanted me—the real me—but I had no model for that kind of healthy and equal relationship. So, I became jealous and fearful that I could lose him. I then turned to my children for opportunities to be needed. They got a double dose of overprotection because I had lost my first dependent.

Later, when Stan went through a fairly typical mid-life crisis, he was struck again with depression, and I had him back. When he was under stress, he made me feel like the most valuable person in the world. Even with the fear and panic that his depression brought, I felt the tie was once again secure.

Viewing myself accurately, within the family of my childhood and the family I had created, was an important step for me in appraising my attitudes and reactions. I needed to look at myself without my disguise of the noble, perfect helper in order to break the stranglehold of my enabling.

8

A QUESTION OF HONESTY

After the trauma of Johnny's illness, I began to see that the way I related to my husband and children involved some subtle form of dishonesty. I hadn't set out to deceive them any more than I had set out to deceive myself, and I am sure I was more effective at deceiving myself than them. But even the attempt at deception resulted in a barrier that was difficult to penetrate.

Not allowing my husband and children to know how insecure I was at times, and how inadequate I felt in my job as wife and mother, was detrimental to them. Because I was uncertain of myself, I felt that I needed to be right.

The need to be right is a very insidious attitude that causes people to become caught up in wars that they feel they have to win. I would begin with the goal of trying to communicate, and somehow end up embroiled in a struggle for victory.

My reluctance to be wrong built a wall that didn't leave an opening through which they could reach me. And it doesn't take long for children to quit trying.

I know that there were times when my children needed advice or comfort but were reluctant to come to me because they felt that I wouldn't understand them. If my children believed that I had only those noble thoughts and pure experiences I pretended to have, it is no surprise that they felt that I would have no basis for understanding them. They also believed that besides being misunderstood, they might possibly be condemned for having troubles. They were like many children who develop an unrealistic picture of the strength and infallibility of their parents. Children can feel so vulnerable and fearful when they approach an apparently omnipotent adult that they hesitate to share their concerns.

In the question of honesty, the problem of low self-esteem rears its ugly head again. A little digging usually reveals that most deceptions are the result of someone's attempt to save face. People are all very adept at communicating misinformation to others so that they appear better or different than they really are.

The hidden agenda is, "I may not be able to get out of you what I want if you know the real scoop," or "You might think poorly of me if you really knew me," or "You might give the job to someone else if you know how incompetent I am." Unworthy people feel that they have to say all the right things, true or untrue, to protect their position, which they may secretly believe they don't deserve.

People with high self-esteem feel good about themselves and don't feel they have to create a cover. If they make a mistake, their own sense of worthiness allows them to admit it, because they know that everyone makes mistakes. Their worthiness is not based on how many times they are right, but on the feeling that they are loved and respected for simply being themselves. People who are overly afraid of rejection and capitulate to that fear can never lead honest, straightforward lives. They do not have the freedom to be themselves and to say what they truly feel.

Enablers develop the habit of keeping thoughts and desires secret for fear of reproach, anger, or rejection. Being this way, an enabler quite naturally has a distaste for, and fear of, confrontation and exposure.

To break the pattern of enabling, it is essential for enablers to be honest and to say what they think and feel.

Often only a very trusted counselor is able to convince someone with low self-esteem that it is safe to expose honest thoughts, but it is an uphill battle even for a professional.

After the incident with the tree, I began to be more honest and open with my husband about everything. I told him about feelings that I had kept buried for years. It gave me the most wonderful sense of relief. I had made an honest woman of myself. The biggest surprise for me, however, came from discovering that I hadn't told him anything he didn't already know. It seems that I had been much more successful at deceiving myself than protecting him.

❀

"Putting your stuff out" is one of my friend's ways of saying communicate. I like this turn of phrase because it is not loaded with the jargon that surrounds the word communication.

Enablers can learn a lot from their co-dependents about putting their stuff out. When Stan was caught up in his own melodrama, he "let it all hang out." I became the tight-lipped juggler whose goal was to keep the situation concealed. I was adept at keeping my feelings and thoughts to myself. I did not want to be exposed as a less than perfect person, and I also tried to manipulate my family's environment to prevent their failings from being exposed. I felt that their flaws reflected on me. I realize now that although my husband and John might have appeared more flawed than I did, they were at least much more honest.

Direct and open communication requires a strong sense of self-worth and a certain amount of fearlessness, neither of which enablers have. Enablers will display resentment at being misunderstood, knowing full well that they are the ones causing the misunderstanding. There is no way people can intelligently and caringly respond to others if they are led to make false assumptions as a result of being given false signals. When enablers won't let their thoughts be known, it is unfair for them to hold others responsible for misunderstanding.

Some enablers are so afraid of rejection that they will enlist a third party to test the water. The third party's job is to determine if it is safe for honest communication. Unwary friends or family members are often caught between two people who refuse to talk directly. It is especially unfortunate when a child is used as an intermediary by parents who don't have the nerve to talk to each other. You have all used go-betweens and you have all been go-betweens.

The legal system functions through mediators. While mediators have their place, the relationship of the enabler and dependent is an intimate one and will not become loving and supportive until the two people involved communicate honestly and directly with each other.

Opening up and being honest is a wonderful gift to give partners, children, or friends. The only way you can really be known is to allow others to know you.

Unfortunately, opening up isn't always a "two-way street." One party can be honest and straightforward in a relationship and have it reciprocated with deception or manipulation. However, to break any established pattern of interaction, someone has to take the initiative and be the first to begin speaking openly and truthfully.

The truth is not just difficult to speak, but it can be equally difficult to hear. If the truth is spoken with genuine respect and caring, however, it is a kindness that can serve as a foundation for the growth of both people.

Being direct with a partner, when honesty has not been a customary part of the relationship, is very frightening.

Your partner may have trouble with the truth, or worse, may tell you the truth about yourself. You must be just as open to hearing the truth as you are to speaking it.

The good news is that speaking honestly and openly can be habit-forming. I find that people generally respond with reciprocal honesty, and those who had been guarded around me started sharing with me instead. Being fallible doesn't make me feel unworthy, as it once did. I am now finding that fallibility is my most powerful connecting link with other people.

Overcoming fear makes way for being honest, and honesty actually helps overcome fear. It takes both courage and faith in what you are doing to say what you think in a non-judgmental way, hoping that it will be accepted with good will.

I have to monitor myself continually so that I don't slide back into defensive dishonesty. But every time I am honest and forthright about the importance of leading a life that focuses on individual responsibility and honesty, I recommit to a new way of being.

❧

At the conclusion of this chapter and four later chapters, I have included worksheets with exercises that may be useful to those readers who recognize themselves as enablers and want to change.

Worksheet #1

SPEAKING HONESTLY

Remember that your goal is not to win, but to establish communication.

1. Make a list of friends and family members with whom you have misunderstandings. Don't overwhelm yourself; choose only two or three people.

2. Decide what you need to do or say to clear up the misunderstanding. Write it down. Practice it if you wish. It is easy to be sidetracked from your original intent when talking to someone.

3. Have no other goal than an honest intent for these people to understand you and for you to understand them. At your own pace, tell them, one at a time, that you want to correct the misunderstanding.

4. Be prepared to listen to whatever it is they have to tell you, and be open to what they say. Their point of view might have important truths that you need to consider.

5. Consciously try to never again misrepresent yourself to others. If someone gets the wrong impression from what you say or do, quickly correct it.

9

ALLOWING OTHERS TO BE
RESPONSIBLE FOR THEMSELVES

Considering the great number of people who make a muddle of their lives, it would appear that it is simple to make life difficult, and difficult to make life simple.

The lucky ones are those who feel essentially loved, respected, and worthy because the majority of their experience with other people has been supportive and caring. They are free to use their time, energy, and intelligence to work and engage in all of the things that bring satisfaction. Their relationships are open and simple, because they can love and be loved freely, without any accompanying games.

It is unfortunate that everyone can't have the best circumstances for a spontaneously happy life. Nevertheless, people have no choice but to accept the physical and mental attributes they have been given and the environments of their childhood. You may have wished for different parents, or to be shorter or taller or smarter, but you are what you are. You simply can't choose the size of your feet or the neighborhood to which your parents move. Your only possibilities for change and control come from the way you react to what you are given.

Reality is this: most people are not blessed with an

optimal combination of innate characteristics and a supportive environment. In the process of growing up, however, they usually come to terms with their less-than-perfect circumstances. They gradually come to accept themselves as they are, adjusting very early to their particular situation. They learn what works best for them and develop their own survival tactics. Everyone walks down this "adjustment pathway."

Traveling along your separate and distinct path is difficult enough, without an enabler blocking the middle of the road.

❧

Often in the past I had wanted to get inside the skins of my children to help them. I felt I was so much more capable of handling their lives than they were. That I was actually denying them their identity never occurred to me. A sense of identity comes with discovering who you are through experience, and self-esteem comes from developing what you have. I had been usurping their identity and chipping away at their self-esteem.

On one occasion, I was participating in a counseling session with Stan and Nina. Nina was going through a particularly difficult time, and I had commented on how sorry I was that I hadn't been able to help her be happier. The counselor turned to me and asked, "Are you responsible for your daughter's happiness?" I sputtered a little, without answering. He then turned to Nina and said, "Do you feel it is your mother's responsibility to keep you happy?" Nina said, "No, of course not." I was surprised that no one but me felt it was my job. Perhaps this attitude was a carry-over from my childhood when I felt the obligation to cheer up my father and mother. If someone wasn't happy, I felt that I might be able to do something about it.

It wasn't just the happiness factor I felt responsible for, either. It was everything about my husband and children's lives. When they hollered help (and even when they didn't), I jumped to the rescue and snatched the problem from their hands.

It took many incidents to make it clear to me that I regularly dove in to assume my children's obligations, preventing them from finding out what worked best for them. I didn't realize that what worked best for me might not work for them at all. The world they lived in was totally different from mine.

I had always thought of Nina as a very smart but disorganized girl. Nina seemed to live in a bubble, paying little attention to the mundane side of existence. So while she was growing up, I always took care of the practical aspects of her life. I believed I was capable of dealing with the everyday matters of which she was not aware. When she left for Boston, I was extremely fearful for her, mainly because I wasn't certain she would be able to take care of the logistics of daily survival, like how to catch the correct bus, where to find a place to live, or how to handle finances. When I visited her at her college in Boston, I was surprised to find that she was doing very well. In addition to doing well in her classes, she had an apartment and a part-time job.

While I was there, we decided to take the train to New York City. At the station, she went to check out schedules. She was looking so puzzled as she read the billboard that I went over to read (translate) it for her. I then asked her how she managed when she first came to the city. She replied, "When you are not around, Mom, I figure it out, but when you are with me, you seem to do things so much more efficiently, I let you do it." Nina admitted that she felt incompetent when she was with me. That hurt! Like every parent, I thought I wanted my children to grow up feeling confident and capable. I had spent years trying to protect my daughter from the troubles of the outside world. The one person she wasn't protected from was me.

Stan had always been aware of my enabling behavior toward the children. He felt that I was too lenient and did too much for them. If he ever said anything critical about one of them, I would come to their defense. Of course, if the children berated their father, I also came to his defense. I protected them from each other.

Stan worried about our children not having as many responsibilities as he felt they should, but when he would try to talk to me about it, I would behave as if he were attacking me and he wouldn't pursue it. He believed me to be a well meaning, caring, mother and he let it go at that. He never transferred his awareness of my being an enabling mother to the recognition that I was also an enabling wife.

I had been an obstacle for my children in many ways. I had always been good at assigning household tasks to my children, but I was never good at following through. If one of them said, "I'll do it later," when the later never came, I would do the chore. If an assignment became inconvenient, difficult, or interfered with their other plans, I rescinded the assignment. It seemed kind, giving, and so much easier. Their lives were busy, and I felt, after all, it was my job to see that the house ran smoothly. I know now that their busy lives should have included consistent responsibility and work.

I wish at that time I had read about the study conducted by George and Caroline Valient of Harvard University regarding the value of work. They found that more than social class, family problems, or intelligence, a child's willingness and capacity to work was the most important factor in predicting his or her mental health as an adult.[1]

Stan had been telling me this in various ways for years, but I always took it as a criticism of my mothering. He had maintained that it is accomplishment that makes people feel good about themselves. It had been hard for me to accept this message coming from Stan, because he had been a slave to accomplishment and he was a prime example of someone who did not feel good about himself. I now recognize that Stan's drive and capacity for hard work are essential to his feeling worthy.

I know how difficult it must be for my children, at this stage, to learn adult skills that have become a habit to most children before they reach adulthood. Children who have never been allowed to develop their own ways for handling the challenges they face are as ill prepared for life as children with an inadequate parental model.

Whatever disability or crisis people endure, they should be allowed the opportunity of developing their own individual means of coping. Adversity is not a license of release from being responsible. Those who lose the use of their legs need to learn to use wheelchairs. Their disability is not justification for not developing all of their possibilities. They are capable of learning to do many of the activities everyone else does. Alcoholics may be prone to addictions, but they can still choose whether or not to take that first drink. People who suffer from depression may still feel despair, but they do have the choice of whether to remain in bed or not. These are their problems—they are the ones who need to develop their own tactic for managing them.

When enablers do everything for people who can't walk, cover up for alcoholics, or give maid service to those who refuse to get out of bed, it makes it hard for their dependents to develop tools for coping with their lot in life. Their enabler becomes one more obstacle, perhaps the biggest obstacle, for them to overcome.

Stan's form of depression is a relatively common malady in contemporary society. Having a propensity to depression was a factor in Stan's life that he needed to consider, understand, accept, and avoid using to exempt himself from the responsibilities of making decisions. He, like everyone else—my children included—needed to accept the unique characteristics of his makeup, acknowledge them, and then make the adjustments necessary to bring his life into agreement with the realities of the world.

I felt so frustrated because I could never alleviate Stan's depression until I finally caught on that dealing with his depression was his job, not mine. I could not make him feel any way he wasn't ready to feel. He did things for his reasons, not mine. I didn't have the power to control either my son's illness or my husband's depression.

In the end, I had to accept that each member of my family is a separate, and very different, individual, and that they are not an extension of me. They have a right to be what they choose—not what I choose.

It seems a strange paradox that standing up for myself and meeting my own needs has actually enhanced the lives of my family.

10

ENABLING

The variety of enabling situations is as infinite as the configurations of all possible relationships: husband-wife, parent-child, friends, lovers, teacher-student, employer-employee, government-constituents and so on. Enabling is a pattern of behavior that afflicts young and old, both genders, and crosses all boundaries.

People in positions of responsibility for others who require some form of help are always in danger of becoming enmeshed in an enabling situation. Women are particularly vulnerable because of their natural maternal instincts and function as family caretakers. But anyone who supports or cares for others due to age or disability is at risk. The line between help that is needed, and help that is enabling is often difficult to discern.

The challenge is to not cross that line from interdependence into enabling-dependence.

❧

People don't fall into enabling while they innocently stroll down the pathway of life. They are not ensnared by those who are weak and dependent. So what is it that makes an enabler willing to take on the additional burden of another person? As I mentioned previously, there is a complex of factors that tend to create enablers.

To begin with, the process of socializing children to become cooperative adults often fosters pleasers. Children are rewarded for doing what they are told to do and for giving in to the mandates of others. Being a "pleaser" is one of the few ways children have to cope with childhood dangers and demands. When giving in to others consistently brings rewards or safety, this way of reacting is reinforced and can be continued into adulthood as enabling. The children who are usually considered good have learned that bending to others, even if it doesn't always bring approval, can often help them escape punishment.

Women, like children, can also find themselves in subservient positions with little direct power over their lives. Accommodating the men in their lives may be necessary for their survival, but it can also give them an avenue for control without upsetting traditional roles.

The rewards that enablers receive for enabling obviously outweigh the troubles and additional work or they wouldn't do it.

Individuals who are capable of assuming the responsibilities of other people are impressive. They get a collective pat on the back and a boost to their self-esteem. They have the opportunity to show the world their superior altruistic nature and their competence. For this reason, enablers work at being virtuous and righteous. They exhibit many seemingly wonderful qualities. They are hardworking, tolerant, capable, courageous, tough, sacrificing, wise, adaptable, forgiving, and loving people. Their multitudinous virtues are enough to gag a normally functioning person.

I don't mean to imply that these traits are not valuable or worthy, but their application does require scrutiny. Each of these virtues has a dark side. One person's exaggerated capabilities can make another person feel incompetent. Forgiveness can breed guilt. Kindness may imply obligation. Tolerance often fosters abuse. Flexibility can take away limits, and strength allows dependency.

While society teaches people to admire the helping traits without question, examining them critically exposes some of their hidden, less admirable aspects. The choice to be an enabler/pleaser/helper may have little to do with any sincere desire to be virtuous.

Maintaining a virtuous personality is essential to an enabler's sense of worth. But it also requires all kinds of sacrifices. Because enablers don't have an honest way to relate to other people, normal interchanges are hindered. Enablers often have to swallow their anger, and suppress or ignore their personal needs. If the enabler is being abused by the dependent, the indignities and hurts are compounded and continue to fester.

This incredible blending of saintly martyr, victim, and superhero is the confusing profile of the enabler.

❦

After I became aware of the way I was relating to other people, especially those close to me, I began to look around to see if I could identify other enablers like me. Focusing solely on enabling relationships, and from my limited vantage point, I saw more than I ever imagined. It was enormously revealing to watch others interact.

❦

Nancy, Stan's secretary, is one of the more obvious enablers. Her twenty-four-year-old son, Tim, manages to land in jail at least once a year. He is never thrown in jail (according to Nancy) for anything major, just piddling infractions of the law. Nancy is very irritated with the police. She believes that they have something against Tim. Over and over again, she bails Tim out. When Stan tells me of Tim's latest brush with the law, I find myself becoming angry at Nancy rather than Tim. She constantly prevents him from learning the lessons he needs to learn if he wants to stay out of jail. Every friend, employer, counselor, and casual acquaintance has advised Nancy to leave him in jail to pay for his offense. She simply cannot bring herself to do it.

When people like Tim are allowed to maintain a worthless lifestyle because they are protected from its natural consequences, it is easy for them to continue depending on someone else to clean up their mess. Their experience of the world is that the world will always accommodate them.

Alcoholics who find a mate who will accommodate their behavior can spend a lifetime without changing. They have someone strong and capable they can depend upon to hold things together, cover for them, and protect them from the penalties of alcoholism. These alcoholics believe themselves to be of victims an uncaring world, when actually they are casualties of an overprotective one.

❦

The children of my friend Jo could win awards if prizes were offered for sloppiness. They walk into the house after fixing the car, throw their greasy shoes on the carpet, sit nonchalantly on the sofa when they are covered with grime, walk into the kitchen and slosh milk into a glass, then drip milk all the way up the stairs and into their bedrooms. Jo patiently follows behind them, trying to undo the damage. Being the family maid doesn't bother her. She considers it her job to be tolerant and gets her reward by graciously accepting whatever comes her way. She believes that the shortest route to sainthood is through martyrdom to a noble cause, and the welfare of her family is a noble cause. So she sits at the kitchen table, staring at the mess, and eats another donut and gains another pound.

People who take on the project of a dependent or a family of dependents have to be hardworking. They care for the house and children, manage the family's business affairs, tend to the needs and desires of dependents, and are sometimes their only financial support. They do the work of two, maybe three, maybe more.

※

Norma, who works in a restaurant that I frequently visit, is both a joy and a pain for me to watch. She seems tireless. When it is slow in the restaurant, she takes time to tell me the latest episode of her family saga.

Norma cleans the house and takes care of her grandchild when she goes home. Her carefree daughter maintains an active social life. Her son, who has gone off into the world to "find himself," needs a little quick cash telegraphed to him now and then. Norma is constantly juggling the family finances because her husband is routinely in and out of work. When I asked her why she took the entire burden on herself, she said, "What can you do?"

A few enablers become accommodating to the point of allowing themselves to be physically abused. The enabling wife of an alcoholic who uses her for his punching bag is a tough lady. She has to be, to be bruised over and over again and still go back for more. It takes courage to walk into a fist. It takes courage to go out in the middle of the night in a dangerous neighborhood checking all of the bars for a delinquent husband. It takes courage to lie to his boss the next day, saying that her husband "has a cold."

This courage, which could be her most precious ally, should be used in defending herself rather than encouraging the vice and weakness of someone else.

※

A casual glance at any dependency relationship is deceptive. The outward cues lead people to believe that the enabler is the one who is stable, wise and exercising good judgment. The dependent's abilities appear questionable. It is ironic that the ones who allow themselves to be used like workhorses can be considered wise. If enablers have all of the answers, why is it so easy for their dependents to cause them to jump through hoops? Is being a drudge, punching bag, patsy or doormat smart?

I was recently involved in a business transaction with an elderly gentleman who, during the course of our interaction, voiced his concern about the future of his business. He mentioned that he had always been the only member of the family considered bright enough to keep the business in the black. He had therefore never included anyone else in company decision-making. He wanted to retire but couldn't; the rest of the family insisted he continue his position because he was wise and had such good judgment. Meanwhile, his family had plush and carefree lives. He may appear to the entire world as having good sense, but it appears to me that his family has outfoxed him.

※

There was something that happened regularly in the family of my childhood, and I have only recently understood its significance. When we had chicken for dinner, my mother always chose the neck. I thought that this was because she preferred it. While visiting her recently, I served dinner and automatically put the chicken neck on her plate. I was startled to hear her say, with the honesty that comes with age, that she hated the neck.

Taking the "neck of the chicken" had obviously been a sacrifice on her part, but it was symbolic of all of our family interactions. I remember that she always chose the neck, the worst part, no matter what goods were being shared or what tasks were being distributed. My mother thought she was being unselfish; actually all that she was being was last. Last should be an equal opportunity position.

A group of friends and I have a regular dinner date. Of course, when a group gets together for a meal, the question of "Where shall we eat?" arises. Beth always says that it doesn't make very much difference to her where we eat. The rest of us, therefore, take turns picking our favorite spots. Consequently, Beth never gets to go where she wants to eat. By being so adaptable, she turns over the fun of choosing to everyone else. It is nice of her to do this, but there is no need. There are plenty of times in this world when people can and should compromise, but continually adapting to others' desires is not compromise. This behavior fosters disregard for the person who chooses not to count, and self-centeredness in the ones who consider they do count. Always adapting to others is not doing yourself, or them, a kindness.

If you should ask an enabler, whatever the circumstances of the enabling, "Why do you take on the load of being your family's caretaker, facilitator, and warrior?" they will look at you as if you don't understand the meaning of love. The question is an insult. To them, the answer is so obvious that they cannot imagine anyone asking. Out of love, they would do anything for those who need them. Enablers cast a powerful protective shield of love over their family and friends, absolutely oblivious to the possibility that they might be smothering them. Even love has its dark side.

❧

Helen, one of the women I work with, has a charming thirty-two-year-old daughter, Jenny, who lives with her. Jenny is Helen's reason for living. It is apparent to anyone enjoying their company how deeply Helen loves her daughter. Helen is constantly taking Jenny on trips, buying her clothes and luxuries, and in general showing her love in every possible way.

Helen is a very happy person. Jenny has a subtle look of desperation in her eyes. She is her mom's beloved toy. Jenny is so in debt to the goodness and giving of her mother that she can never leave her. That Helen can't see and feel Jenny's desperation has made me question the nature of real love. Helen will give Jenny anything, except what Jenny really wants: her freedom and independence.

When you are not hampered by your own insecurities and fears, you are able to more accurately assess the love you feel for others. While it might break your hearts to let go of someone, if you can honestly look that person in the eye and say, "I want you to be all you can, the best you can, with or without me," you know your love is genuine.

❧

One of my husband's friends, Ray, loves his sons very much and would do anything for them, but he can't see that his own insecurity is crippling them. Ray is a man of many abilities. He is capable of figuring out almost any task from plumbing to home accounting. When he describes inter- actions with his sons about household odd jobs, there are two themes that consistently emerge. One is his grumbling about how he has to do everything for them, and the other is his laughing at the stupid mistakes they make in doing simple tasks—always leaving him in the position of having to complete their botched projects.

I have been around Ray when he has been advising his sons about work on their cars. Before, in the middle of, and after the project, Ray gave shrewd advice on how it could be done better, differently, or more effectively. He seemed unable to restrain himself from butting into their projects. Any outside observer can see why he ends up doing all of the work around his house. I know his sons well, and Ray always having one more suggestion has taken a heavy toll on their self-esteem. In the guise of helper, their father has succeeded only in making them feel incompetent.

❧

An enabler's master virtue is to be forgiving. "To err is human and to forgive divine." It is easy to guess who gets which label when an enabler and a dependent clash. Such platitudes lend both comfort and smug pride to offended enablers. Pretending to forgive (and I say pretend because real forgiveness is not what enablers offer) can heap enough guilt on a dependent to cow him for a lifetime.

It seemed my mother forgave my father over and over again, because she always allowed him back into her good graces. I suspect that only after his death did she truly forgive him, if then.

11

A MATTER OF SELF-ESTEEM

When I was a child, my mother always appeared perfect to me. As an adult, I realize she was just a good person making the best of her circumstances. But in my early years, it seemed as though she confronted whatever came her way with superlative strength. I believed I could be like her and handle any problems I had with that same quality of perfection and strength. What I really believed was that my life would have no problems.

I intended to have everything when I grew up—a successful, adoring husband, clever children, a split-level in the suburbs and perennial good health.

This innocent belief was probably not too different from the hopes of many young girls. Believing that it is possible to live a perfect life is a common fantasy of youth. Too often, this fantasy proves to be an impenetrable barrier to growth.

Many children are not encouraged to look at life realistically. I'm not referring to setting high standards or believing that one should strive to do worthwhile things. I'm referring to the unrealistic expectation that normal life is free of problems. My generation considered the virtuous woman, the loving wife and mother, their ideal. Today's youth are more likely to envision a different type of perfection, but they are no better prepared to face adult life than my generation. They are just being led through a different maze. Modern youth have cut their teeth on the fast-paced, multi-colored medium of television, which portrays everyone as beautiful, slim, and living the life of a Coca-Cola ad—fun and exciting. The model of the successful woman is now one who leads a busy social life while managing a brilliant professional career.

Now that technological society has given people a window to the world, they can also view the best in every field. Present day culture has come to idolize those who excel in the arts, sciences, politics, and athletics. They are put on ridiculously high pedestals and their special talents and attractiveness are equated with personal worthiness. Constantly seeing people with outstanding beauty and special gifts can make young people feel grossly inadequate.

It is hard for the present crop of young people to deal with pimples, braces, knock-knees, fat, and immature talent while being bombarded daily with the beautiful and rich who live life from thrill to thrill in the fantasy world of television. Society fosters the idea that each young woman should be beautiful, each young man an action hero, and that growing old is unseemly. Does anyone wonder that self-esteem is a monumental problem in our society?

A good many people have the added misfortune of coming from poorly functioning families, in which the parents not only don't actively work to build self-esteem but, indeed, foster a feeling of inferiority in their children. Developing a realistic view of life is crucial if you are to accept yourself as a worthy individual. No one can measure up to a standard that isn't authentic. Who can constantly be young, energetic, benevolent, and brilliant?

Clinging to a childhood belief that I could have a perfect life and be an outstanding mother and wife served as a stumbling block to effective marriage and parenthood. Anything that transpired during our daily family interaction that did not fit my imaginary picture looked like failure to me. The farther my family's reality was from my naïve view of what it should be, the greater my loss of self-esteem. I erroneously believed that I could create the perfect home. When I couldn't create my fantasy, I felt incompetent.

Poor self-esteem is the principal factor in enabler-dependent relationships. Those who for whatever reasons feel unworthy need to develop a realistic view of what human living is about.

Since low self-esteem is at the heart of enabling, enablers need to reach into the dark corners of their minds and probe the feelings and beliefs they have about themselves. It is important to identify the source of any behavior they want to change.

To understand the connection between low self-esteem and enabling, think again of Ray, who wouldn't allow his sons to do anything completely on their own, without his expert advice. Ray's insistence on being the expert is more symptomatic of his poor self-esteem than of his great expertise. His own father, who is now in his seventies, still chuckles about the stupid things Ray did as a youth. He treats Ray as though he were a blundering boob. So Ray is passing the neurosis on to his sons—who will pass it on to their sons, ad infinitum. Unless someone in the chain has the insight and courage to break it, the situation could continue indefinitely.

If Ray could distance himself enough to view his interaction with his sons objectively, I believe that he would understand the effect his enabling is producing. He then might try to discover why he feels a constant need to show his superiority. Ray needs to recognize his low self-esteem and identify its source. He could then allow his sons to learn to feel capable and independent, and he could also begin to do the things that would help him develop and enhance his own self-esteem. All Ray really wants is to feel good about

himself and to prove to his sons that he is competent—
since he will never be able to prove it to his own father.

When enablers look clearly at the factors that have con-
tributed to their feelings of unworthiness, they will recognize that most of those feelings have been created as a result
of the manipulation of others who likewise felt unworthy.
Enablers need to learn how to replace the negative pictures
of themselves that they have acquired, along with the
deceptive myths about an ideal life.

Once enablers begin to live lives based on realistic
expectations and actual possibilities, they find that real
life is much more rewarding than childhood fantasies ever
were.

Worksheet #2

KNOWING YOURSELF

1. List all the qualities, good or bad, which you believe describe you—not what others have said, but what you in your heart know to be true. This should be a long list. For example:

    I am female
    A perfectionist
    Child of an alcoholic
    Love to read
    Want everyone to like me
    Near-sighted
    Work well with my hands
    I am tall, etc.

    Add to your list whenever you think of anything else that describes you.

2. Put a plus sign next to all of the items that you wouldn't want to change if you could, because they are positive traits, or because you simply like these qualities in yourself.

    These are strengths—feel good about them.

3. Go over your list and star all of the things that can't be changed, for example, *I am tall*. Then, taking one item at a time, begin to let it be OK to have these qualities you can't change. Start with

an item that is not overly threatening, and tell yourself several times each day that it is acceptable to be this way. Remind yourself that it is not realistic to expect yourself to be perfect, or to believe that the circumstances of your life will always be ideal. To be satisfied with yourself and your life, you have to willingly accept yourself as you really are.

4. Put all the items that are not starred—those that can be changed—on a new list, and keep it for use in a later exercise.

12

COMMITTING TO CHANGE

Living has often been likened to the flow of a river, because its current is such an apt analogy for lives as they move through time. People are continually tumbling along, bending, narrowing when they must, widening when they can, but rushing in an ever-changing path to an unknown destination. In spite of life's constant ebb and flow, there are many people who become so rigidly attached to familiar things that their lives more fittingly resemble stagnant ponds.

Perhaps the most important difference between those who flow through life and those who stagnate is their ability to adapt to change. People who live their lives in a fixed, well-defined manner are traumatized when an incident occurs which disturbs their pattern. Events that force a change in their lives more often cause them to spend their energies fighting to stabilize and protect the status quo, rather than concentrating that energy to master their changed situation. They will work to save what they have been, even when they aren't sure that it is worth saving.

The ability to change and the willingness to change are both important factors in living a more stimulating and interesting life. K. Warner Schaie of Pennsylvania State University conducted a study of 2,000 adults, which correlated a person's ability to adjust to change with mental alertness. He found higher mental acuity among those older members of the group who lived more flexible life-styles and adapted easily—that is, those who varied their routines and were open to new and additional activities. He concluded that people who do not adapt well to changing situations are at the greatest risk of losing their intellectual abilities.[2]

❦

Change is inevitable. It is the only constant that can be counted on. The more adroit you are at adapting and capitalizing on change, the richer and more exciting your life becomes. Viewed in this way, it is surprising that people will spend so much energy avoiding change. Often the best thing that can happen to you comes from a change that you may have spent a good bit of your life resisting. Fight it or will it, change happens. You can choose to suffer over what "once was" or welcome what is now to be had.

Enablers can choose to quit enabling. Yet consummate enablers who are stripped of their dependents by some external force or event don't really give up enabling. They transfer their attention to the next needy person in line. If there are no other relatives or friends who are willing to apply for the vacancy, they put their considerable skills on hold and take a vacation until the post can be filled.

Giving up enabling requires more than having the universe remove a dependent from your household. It requires a conscious decision to alter the way you interact with other people, and particularly with people who slide easily into dependent roles.

The conscious decision to quit encouraging the dependency of others demands real commitment. Once you recognize yourself as an enabler and determine not to relate to people from a position of being needed, it is necessary to get out of the stagnant pond and go jump into the river. It is time to move, to be flexible, to grow, and to change.

Breaking the enabling habit requires:

1. Recognition

2. Admission of responsibility

3. Commitment to quit enabling

Recognition

The biggest barrier to change for most people is refusing to believe or accept they have anything that needs changing. So the primary foundation for change has to be a realization that a change is needed. This realization, whether you like it or not, brings with it a certain amount of responsibility. When people are reluctant or afraid to even look at an issue, it is generally because they really don't want to be under an obligation to act.

There is no way to force enablers to look at themselves objectively. If they refuse to recognize their enabling, they can't be helped any more than alcoholics who refuse to admit they have a drinking problem. But should enablers ever be able to catch an impartial vision of themselves in action, they will feel impelled to stop enabling.

Commitment to change is only possible for the enablers who take that first important step of identifying themselves as enablers. Those who recognize that they are enablers will, in small ways, begin to change without conscious effort. Just this awareness will trigger change. These enablers have developed a new perception of enabler-dependent relationships, and they can no longer deny their complicity. Watching themselves respond in an enabling manner will make them feel foolish, a condition in which enablers are

more accustomed to seeing their dependents than themselves.

Admission of responsibility

Recognizing that one is an enabler is one thing. Bringing
the matter into the open for discussion is quite another.
But exposing enabler-dependent behavior is a crucial step
to initiating a new way of interacting. Having the spotlight
on both the enabler's and the dependent's conduct inter-
feres with their ability to continue as they were. The jig is
up. Once the parties involved identify the game, it loses its
power.

The first step of admitting responsibility is to initiate a
dialogue with your dependent, clearly stating and acknowledging the problem of your enabler-dependent dynamic.
This solitary action will precipitate a change, however
minor, in the future responses of your dependent. Then
you will be put to the test of reacting differently to their
response—causing them to counter differently—and this
spiraling change creates a new form of interaction. By
clearing yourself of your usual way of operating, you open
the way to a new and more direct form of personal interaction.

Commitment to quit enabling

In its ability to produce sweaty palms and heart palpi-
tations, the word commitment is second only to the word
change. When the two are combined, they can produce
powerful resistance. Change is stressful to everyone.
Moreover, commitment obligates you to constancy, a
promise to be faithful and consistent in your actions. So
committing to change can become a double threat filled
with ambiguity. It is an obligation to pursue the as-yet-un-
known truths about life and about yourself. Because of this
double challenge, an enabler has to want to change. There

are many effective techniques for breaking the enabling habit, but they are all useless until a fundamental commitment to quit enabling is made.

Commitments are serious. But it is a pity that society has made the idea of commitment seem so scary. The word itself has become synonymous with burden. To dedicate yourselves to a goal that will bring greater fulfillment to you and those you love should be life giving rather than deadening. When you choose to give up an enabler-dependent relationship for a mutually supportive one, it should be approached as a pleasurable challenge rather than a grim chore. It can be exhilarating, and it can bring new excitement.

Why people are afraid of commitment is no mystery, especially when it represents commitment to change. They don't know what will happen should they begin something new, something that can't be reversed. Good or bad, the present is known, and the known is secure. They have already accommodated to it.

The wife of an alcoholic may have the security of knowing that her husband will be spending his evenings passed out on the couch at home. Who knows what he would do if he became a fully functioning man? He might find more creative ideas about how to spend an evening that would not include her. That is threatening and it may feel safer not to do anything, even though her situation is miserable.

The man who ridicules his wife about being socially inept, although annoyed with her clinging to his arm and not mingling at social gatherings, knows that she will never stray very far. Should she improve her self-image, he will no longer be able to control her social contacts. He may feel insecure about her loyalty if she developed her own set of friends.

If you commit yourself to developing a life based on

something besides having others need you, you must be willing to face whatever happens to them as a result of that commitment. You must have faith in yourself and trust that you have the ability to create a rewarding life for yourself under any conditions, with or without your dependents.

The willingness to accept whatever happens as a result of any shifts in your relationships gives you the courage to change. It is a matter of trusting that the universe will do its part if you do yours.

Luckily, you are not required to live your entire life at once. You live one day at a time. And that is the way your commitments should be tackled, one day at a time. Once you decide how you want to live, there is ample opportunity to practice. Each day is practice for the next. All you need to worry about is being responsible for the decision of the moment. Living moment by moment and having dominion over the moment can produce dramatic long-term changes in your life. In moving through life, all you have to do is make a commitment to alter your direction very slightly, and then follow that course in order to end up at a different and healthier destination.

Because change is a lifelong process, I knew that all of the new practices I had started would trigger growth in me, and they have. I wasn't trying to reach a specific goal; I was trying to develop a different way of relating to people.

Worksheet #3

CHANGING YOURSELF

1. Review the list you made for Worksheet #2, Item 4. This is the list of the characteristics that you identified as having the potential to be changed.

2. Decide which of these traits you would like to change, and think about why you would like them changed.

3. Choose one item from your list that seems the most simple to change and make a commitment to change it. Do not concern yourself with how you will accomplish the change—just make the commitment.

4. Tell someone you trust about this commitment. You may think that this is nobody's business, that you need only make this commitment to yourself, but research indicates that people who make their goals known are more likely to achieve them.[3] Social pressure keeps you honest with yourself.

5. List three things that you can begin to do differently which will move you toward your goal. Be realistic; select changes that you can make successfully. For example, if you can't stop yourself from reminding your son every evening after dinner to do his homework, then: 1. when dinner

is over get out of the house and go for a walk,
2. find a project you enjoy and do it in any room
except the one where your son is, 3. call a friend
on the telephone at this time.

13

FACING FEAR

When enablers make the commitment to stop enabling, they step right into the middle of their personal fears. There is a real possibility that altering their behavior may represent the end of a relationship. These warriors, who can firmly face everyone else's demons and fight with sword in hand to protect others, become paralyzed to take any steps when faced with their own demons.

The issue of personal esteem is so subtle, deep, and frightening to look at that most people will not acknowledge it as a factor when they face the fear of losing a relationship.

Doubting your own worth is what makes most of you lose faith in the strength of your ties. Ideal ties between family members are based on love, respect, and shared goals. Feeling unworthy of your family's love can cause you to be afraid of losing their support. Making yourselves indispensable to your family members is an unfortunate but effective way of keeping them around when you are not sure whether they are with you out of love or necessity. Enablers' greatest fears are that their dependents will leave if they dissolve the dependencies they have created.

Enablers and dependents develop relationships based on mutual poor self-esteem. They come from positions of personal insecurity and count on each other's insecurity to keep the relationship stable. Surprisingly, these relationships, while being grim or sometimes tempestuous and painful, are very stable—until one of the participants begins to work toward improving his or her self-image. When either the enabler or the dependent tries to break the cycle, the deep hidden fears and feelings of insecurity surface.

Neither party in the relationship may be willing to seek counseling because they fear that the only solution to their enabling-dependence is to dissolve the relationship. Separation, however, is not usually the best remedy. When partners separate without dealing with underlying attitudes and insecurities, they will most likely re-create the same situation with new partners. They can be doubly demoralized and confused if they thought that changing partners was the answer, only to find themselves in the same type of relationship again.

It is not the relationship that is the culprit so much as the couple's method of relating. When both participants are willing to learn about themselves and modify the way they interact, their changed responses can precipitate growth in each other and alter the dynamics of their relationship in a positive way.

Making yourself happy now, in the present circumstance, is the real prize. It doesn't mean that either one of you or both might not wish for better or different circumstances, but better or different are more likely to be created from a position of happiness.

When both the enabler and the dependent want to stop their co-dependence, the chances are good that their bond will become stronger from their mutual commitment to improve themselves and their relationship.

When enablers are involved with hardcore dependents, they may fear that they are only truly wanted as caretakers—that when they give up enabling, their partners will dump them for someone who will continue to take care of them. They may be right. I believe that the enablers' new self-esteem, gained in the process of working for a more rewarding life, will carry them through the loss and keep them from attracting the same sort of people to repeat their former co-dependent relationships.

The ability to distinguish an enabler-dependent relationship from one built on love, caring, and mutual work toward common goals is very important in understanding the dynamics of enabling.

Partners in a loving relationship are secure in the belief that they could survive separately. It is out of love, not need, that they choose to be together. They need each other only because they love each other. This is quite different from dependence, which is based on a feeling of deficiency and the fear of being alone. In a loving relationship, the partners serve as a cheering section for one another—knowing that the goal is to improve the quality of both of their lives. Combined, they form a dynamic unit. By contrast, co-dependents, while feigning support, are simply fostering needs.

These two types of partnerships look very different to an outside observer.

To illustrate, I'll describe the situation of a wife, with grown children, who wants to return to college after many years.

A supportive husband would:

» tell his wife that she is capable

» offer to help with the household duties

» offer financial support

>> not make her feel guilty about spending time on herself

>> celebrate when she graduates.

The husband who wants to foster need would:

>> tell his wife that school is very difficult, and he is worried that she can't compete

>> tell her that she already has more to do than she can handle, and he doesn't want her under that much stress

>> begin creating more tasks for her to do around the house

>> make her feel selfish (and foolish—at her age!)

In contrasting scenarios for a couple with a new baby:

The wife who wishes to support her husband as a partner in parenting will:

>> show her husband how to feed and diaper the baby

>> teach him all of the little tricks she has figured out to keep the baby contented

>> encourage special times for father and child to be alone together.

The wife who wants to foster dependence of both the father and baby will:

» avoid leaving the baby alone with its father

» withhold all of her knowledge so that she becomes indispensable to both the father and the baby

» put herself in the middle, so they both need her around as a go-between.

In these two examples, the principles are the same: Partners in a supportive relationship have high self-esteem and feel worthy of being loved. They feel good about themselves and want their mates to feel the same.

Enablers and dependents who feel unworthy seek to bolster their poor self-images by standing on the shoulders of their partners. They place the partners in the position of being less, rather than more, diminishing their partner's already poor self-respect. It is a downward spiral for both parties.

For those who have strong feelings of worthlessness, attracting and keeping a mate and clinging to children, parents, or friends is often an exercise in manipulating the others into positions of need. Even the thought of altering the needing interaction in such relationships produces a fear of losing the dependent. Enablers may be reluctant to commit to altering their behavior because they know that their relationships are not soundly based on mutual respect.

There are many husbands who, with professions of great love, bring home chocolates to their dieting wives. Many wives, with loving kindness, cook oversized meals for their overweight husbands, and then feel hurt if their husbands don't show appreciation for their efforts by eating everything. Once the underlying principles are understood, it is easy to distinguish enabling behavior from loving behavior.

Love relationships are based on one doing what is best, in the long run, for the people one loves. Need relationships are in fact self-centered, with the pretense of concern for the partner.

❧

Women are often subject to even greater fears than men. The loss of a mate may represent the loss of security, home, income, and status. A woman is likely to be programmed to believe that she needs a man, and she sets about creating a situation in which a man needs her. Should the enabler then want to change her relationship from an enabling one to a loving one, she has to face the possibility of losing both her emotional support and her economic protection.

While twenty-first century culture is slowly moving toward balancing the scale of sexual power, facing the problems of employment, housing, and safety in a "man's world" is a definite concern for women. For a woman to feel at the mercy of a male-dominated world is not a totally irrational fear.

I have often thought about my parents' relationship. As a child, I often became angry with my mother because I couldn't understand why she wouldn't leave my father when he was drinking. I see the situation differently now. She had six children during the Depression. It was a time when it was not only difficult but almost impossible for a woman to obtain employment. Had she succeeded in finding a job, it would have paid very little. My mother's survival, and that of her children, was dependent on the farm that my father owned, and later, upon his rentals in the city. Taking care of him and picking up the ball when he dropped it had to be done in order to feed her children.

It would have been better for my father if she could have let him fall on his face. Had my mother let him suffer the consequences of his irresponsibility, however, my father could have lost his farm. That might have been a "growth experience" for him, but it would have been devastating for my mother and us children.

My mother, my sisters, my daughter and I have all experienced the frustration of not being able to exert direct power over our own lives—of having to check with the significant men in our lives to make important (and often unimportant) decisions. Over the centuries, women, not having direct power or influence, have resorted to cajoling, cunning manipulation, and subtle rewarding and punishing—all sorts of "behind the scenes" actions. Now that society is working toward giving women more power, women are unskilled in using it, and easily revert to techniques of manipulation (such as enabling) that seemed the only option for their mothers.

For women to break the pattern of enabling, they must give up trying to maintain control by manipulation and begin to exert the power that society is now offering. Women are finally having more choices. It is time for them to stop operating as if their circumstances were the same as those of their mothers and realize that in present day society, the opportunities for direct power are growing.

Worksheet #4

CHALLENGING FEAR

Most people who automatically respond to difficult situations by enabling continue to do so because they are afraid of what may happen if they quit. If you want to quit enabling you must break through this fear.

The best way to conquer fear is to understand the fear so thoroughly that it loses its power to intimidate you. Use this worksheet as a guide to attempt a new approach. For purposes of the exercise, choose a relatively innocuous fear relating to your enabling—then:

1.   Dissect it! Don't generalize. Be specific.

For instance, you are afraid to allow your son to miss school, although he consistently misses the school bus, so you get him up, practically dress and feed him, load him into the car and drive him to school. You do this month after month. Why? What exactly are you afraid of if you quit doing it? On a notepad quickly list what you are afraid might happen if you quit being his watchdog. This list should include everything you can think of that might be the source of your fear.

Example:

» *Joey will get behind in his schoolwork and be held back a year.*

> » *He will take the opportunity to drop out of school.*

> » *He will start spending his time with kids who use drugs.*

> » *Joey is lazy—if I don't push him, there's no telling where he will end up.*

> » *He will get in trouble with the school officials.*

2. Are your fears justified?

Consider each item thoughtfully and examine it closely. Try to determine the actual roots of your fear. Are they realistic possibilities? or just habits of thought, or a symptom of your own stress? Cross off all the items that just won't happen. (For example, if he doesn't use drugs, it is doubtful that staying home will start him in on that path!) Now you have a list of realistic causes of your fear, and some possible outcomes that could really happen if you stop enabling.

3. From the items remaining on your list, select the single fear that is the most potent in motivating you to assume someone else's responsibility (in this case your son's), and focus on that fear.

Continuing the example, you are now in the habit of driving Joey to school because he always gets up late, and he knows you will do it. You hate being a taxi service, but you have decided that what you are really afraid of is that he will get in trouble with the school officials.

4. Looking at this singular fear, imagine all of the possibilities for disaster that could occur should you change the way you respond. Make a list of these. Example:

    I will be summoned by the school officials to explain Joey's absences or why he always misses first period.
    Then what?

    I'll suffer the intense embarrassment of having to explain his irresponsibility, and why I won't do something about it (meaning intervene by enabling).
    Then what?

    I will be warned that if he continues to miss school they will send a truant officer for him.
    Then what?

5. Push this as far as you need to in order to face down your fears. Carry each horrible possibility step by step further, always asking yourself, "what then?"

    The school will send a truant officer to pick him up. I will feel totally humiliated, but then so will Joey.
    Then what?

    Here's what: Joey probably will start catching the bus all by himself.
    You may feel humiliated or mean when you

refuse to continue enabling; it's true. But remember, it is not you who is missing the bus.

When your dependents see that you mean business, they most likely will begin to take care of themselves. You'll likely discover that the sky will not fall when you refuse to continue the role of surrogate person. Dissecting every fear and taking it to its end will give you enough information to make an intelligent decision independent of fear.

6. Decide on the best long-term outcome for your dependent—and yourself.

In the example we have been following, the obvious long-term goal is for Joey to be the person getting up on time and getting himself to school. But there is much more to it than that. The enabling mother has to approach the situation with the conviction that she is achieving a breakthrough for herself. Whatever enabling situation you may be caught in, always remember that you are as disadvantaged by your enabling behavior as is your dependent. Frame goals that specify the best outcome for both you and your dependent.

[A final note: Sometimes a problem like Joey's is not caused or encouraged by an enabler. If Joey actually were using drugs, or suffering a physical illness or endogenous depression, you as a parent, with the support of family, school, and community, would have a responsibility to intervene and get him the help he needs.]

14

KEY TO CHANGE

Controlling your automatic enabling response is the key to transforming your way of relating to people.

This is easy to say but difficult to accomplish, because the way you typically respond to people and situations has become part of your personality and is one of the qualities that defines you.

Like it or not, other people have already classified you by the way you characteristically respond: "She will get hysterical." "He will be livid." "She will never speak to me again." "He will become despondent." "She will help." "You won't get any help from him."

By the time you become an adult, the way you respond to other people and situations has become established and is practically automatic.

What lays beneath your style of responding are your gut emotions, which are tightly intertwined and fused with how you feel about yourself in relationship to the world.

It is nearly impossible to disregard feelings that have essentially become part of you and that you clearly experience. It is equally hard to manufacture feelings you don't have. Have you ever had someone say to you, "Oh, you shouldn't feel that way," and you knew that this was absurd, because there was no possible way you could feel differently from how you felt? True feelings can't be changed by force of will. This is both good and bad. It's good in that your feelings are the most valuable tool you have for understanding yourself. It's bad because of the controlling influence feelings have for triggering counterproductive responses.

As an enabler, your response is rooted in your feelings of unworthiness, and since the enabler-dependent relationship is an unhealthy response to feelings of low self-esteem, choosing a more appropriate response is vital to the development of higher self-esteem in both enabler and dependent.

Whether you realize it or not, both you and your dependents have repeatedly chosen your present way of reacting to each other by giving way to the pressure of your feelings. Now it will be necessary to make a conscious effort to retrain your responses. While acknowledging the way you feel, you must re-choose the way you respond. This is your key to change. While your feelings may not be wholly under your control, your actions are.

Consciously changing your reactions will initiate a thoroughgoing change in your interactive pattern.

About feelings

While feelings are a formidable power to be reckoned with, they can be incredibly unreliable guides. Too often, feelings are based on inaccurate perceptions of other people or situations, eliciting a course of action from you that is totally unwarranted.

The biggest interference you will face in truly trying to understand other people is assuming that everyone else feels as you do. Psychologists call this projection.

In projection, other people serve as mirrors. When you look at them you see yourself and believe them to have the same feelings and attitudes you hold. Believing a particular thing about someone else tells you much more about yourself than it does about that person. What you believe about other people can be very misleading. No one ever truly knows what another person is thinking or feeling. You only know what you think and what you feel. They may tell you what they are thinking or feeling, but you have no guarantee that it is true. It may or may not be. You are at the mercy of their self-perception and honesty.

To illustrate this concept, a married woman who wishes to be free again and is not able to admit it to herself may project this feeling onto her husband. She sees all sorts of signs that her husband wants out of the marriage. He, on the other hand can be totally oblivious to her discontent, because he is happy and projects his happiness onto her in the same way that she has projected her discontent onto him.

In this instance, she is watching for signs of discontent in her husband, and accuses him of not loving her anymore and wanting to be rid of her. He on the other hand is bewildered and confused and starts bringing her flowers to reassure her. She finds this very suspicious and additional evidence. Her own feelings have led her astray. Unaware, she is dishonestly dealing with her feelings on the wrong front.

Apart from being blind about the source of a feeling, you can also be off beam concerning the target of the feeling and aim your action or response toward the wrong object.

This is displacement and it means transferring your feelings about one thing onto another. Often when it is too dangerous or uncomfortable to respond directly to the source of a feeling, the response is aimed at someone or something else. Getting rid of anger in an unrelated context toward an innocent recipient is an all too familiar reaction. The anecdote of the man who comes home and kicks the dog because he is angry with his boss is a clichE9, but superbly illustrates the concept. Most abused spouses and children are the victims of displaced anger. Their abusers are usually reacting to pent up anger from having been abused themselves in their childhood.

Enabling is on the list of displaced responses. You are displacing your needs onto someone else.

❦

Another important response to either a painful or inconvenient feeling is that of denial. Enablers also employ this technique. In their solicitous attitude toward the requirements of dependents, they deny their own needs, literally asserting (and believing) that they have no needs.

A good example of an inconvenient and socially inappropriate feeling is that which offspring hold toward parents. Scores of people deny they ever felt any resentment toward their parents. Resenting one's parents is considered ungrateful, and is censured by society. Yet you would not be human if you had not resented your parents at some time or other, for real or imagined wrongs. You can refuse to admit it and even come to believe it isn't true, but denial has got you by the throat.

The reason it is important to monitor your feelings for any tinges of latent denial is that denial of reality blocks personal growth.

In this instance, accepting normal childhood resentment frees you to see your parents realistically, and accept and love them for who they are, clearing the way for a better relationship.

❦

Using feelings as a reason and excuse for unacceptable and often unlawful behavior is the most ominous by-product of misdirected feelings. People justify all sorts of atrocious behavior claiming they were overpowered by their feelings.

A mother who strikes her son across the face and justifies it by saying, "I'm sorry but you made me angry" is not off the hook. It may be that her anger was the source of the blow, but feeling angry and striking her child are not the same thing. Anger is a feeling and striking is a response. While she may not have been able to control her anger, she did not have to react by hitting. Her response was optional.

With intent, time, effort and practice, negative responses can be replaced by positive ones. The man who is upset from a bad day at the office can cool his anger by jogging around the block instead of kicking the dog. The woman whose child does something that makes her angry can send him to his room and go drink a cup of tea.

Enablers, too, can develop tactics for responding more appropriately. If you honestly look at yourself and accept the feelings that are the source of your enabling, you will be free to consciously decide on suitable responses, rather than being at the mercy of your automatic reactions.

About responses

I have painted a very bleak picture of the virtually unassailable nature of feelings. But luckily, in addition to the feeling factor, humans are blessed with a thinking component. You have the ability to reason and make choices under the direction and supervision of your mind rather than your feelings. You can thoughtfully and willfully control your responses. You can plan a course of action and rehearse your response, so that you are prepared. To begin reacting differently will be one of the most difficult challenges of your life. Nevertheless, it can be done. It has been done. The worksheet at the conclusion of this chapter has been designed to help you with this mission.

If, after thoughtfully reading the earlier part of this book, you have figured out why you are enabler, and you have made a conscious commitment to quit enabling, you need to launch a campaign to control your reactions.

Changing the way you act, even an insignificant action, can have an influence on how you feel. One of the rewards you will reap from changing your responses is that you will begin to cultivate new and different feelings. The following two studies illustrate this point.

☙

Dr. Sara Snodgrass of Skidmore College studied the effects of modes of walking on the mood of the walker. She instructed some of the walkers in her study to take long purposeful strides. A second group was told to use a natural gait. The third group was told to shuffle along, looking downward. The mood of the first two groups remained stable, but the shufflers reported that they felt fatigued and depressed during their walk. Dr. Snodgrass's research seems to agree with earlier studies, which indicated that taking on the appearance of a particular mood can affect people by bringing on the thoughts and emotions associated with that mood.[4] Looking sad, for example, can produce a feeling of sadness. Acting angry can feed rage.

Obviously, there are many factors that contribute to the way you feel. Simply altering your behavior is not the complete answer, but it is part of the answer. Behavioral psychologists have shown that changing your behavior can affect your perceptions and beliefs, and these, in turn, are powerful conditioners of mood, self-image, and feelings. Feelings and responses, therefore, are reciprocal. Counseling may give you direction and insight, but working to monitor your behavior gives you something to do—and takes away your feeling of powerlessness.

❧

Darby Prince and Peter Dowrick of the University of Alaska videotaped interviews with thirty-two women who were mildly to moderately depressed. Then they took the videotapes of sixteen of these women and edited them down to only the shots in which the women were smiling and animated. All of their sad, depressive behavior was deleted. The women then watched themselves laughing and gesturing in these edited tapes. At the end of two weeks, the women who watched the tapes of themselves in a happy mood showed less depression than the remaining women, whose interviews were replayed unedited.[5]

Changing physical patterns or routines can initiate different ways of feeling, which initiate different ways of responding, which initiate different ways of feeling, and on it goes.

Exercising a choice over how you respond to your conditions puts a great deal of control into your hands. Because behavior is part of the dynamic of relationships, if you alter your behavior in a positive way, your relationships have to improve.

The short and long of it

Psychologist Albert Ellis, founder of the Institute of Rational Emotive Therapy in New York, tried to determine why so many clients who seek help actually sabotage their own efforts toward self-improvement. After making a long list of the sources of client failure, he concluded that many of his clients opted for short-term goals, rather than sticking to a long-range plan that would serve them better.[6] For example, the woman who drives her son to school because he continues to miss the bus is foregoing a long-term solution to the problem, in order to meet her short-term goal of getting the child to school today.

❦

Responding immediately to a feeling without concern for where that response may lead is not controlling the response beneficially. The goal for enablers is to separate their feelings from their responses—not deny their feelings, but gain control of where their feelings are leading.

Worksheet #5

RESPONDING APPROPRIATELY

1. Choose one situation in which you know your enabling is detrimental.

   For example, calling the high school to cover for your son who ditches school regularly, or giving in to your two-year-old child when she throws a tantrum.

2. Study the situation and then determine the best solution in the long run.

   For your son to quit ditching, or your daughter to quit throwing tantrums.

3. Design a strategy to alter your behavior so that you can reach the long-range goal.

   Perhaps you allow the school to punish your son, as they would anyone else's son whose parent didn't cover for him. Play music you like or read an engrossing book so that you can live through your daughter's tantrums without giving in to her demands.

4. Monitor your reactions day by day so you begin to do only those things that will achieve your long-range goal.

   Change doesn't happen overnight. Practice until the change is a habit. Consistency is what matters.

15

LIVING DIFFERENTLY

For people who have never known the pleasure that comes from an honest, direct, self-actualizing life, the drama of high tragedy may lend a feeling of being alive. There is something rather thrilling in the rush of adrenalin that comes from being upset. It elevates jaded senses and gives a burst of meaning to what may be an otherwise boring life.

When trouble erupts in a household, enablers have an opportunity to launch into action. Trouble means added responsibilities for them, giving them more to do. Trouble can cause upsetting interchanges within the family, allowing enablers to have more personal contact with each family member. Most importantly, trouble brings enablers a heightened feeling of competence and self-esteem. Even the inner turmoil, fear, and resentment enablers feel is more exciting than the blahs.

For dependents, floundering in devastation helps them maintain the role and mystique of being misunderstood. Melancholy has a certain glamour about it, and the pathos of unfulfilled longing can bring a bittersweet pleasure which dependents are reluctant to surrender.

Enablers and dependents both may enjoy the drama of their tragedy too much to give it up. Or they may dread what seems worse—boredom or indifference from those they care about. Unless enablers are willing to replace their

hyper-dramatic life script with a more personally fulfilling one, they will find it hard to resist spending their time
rescuing others.

Giving up an old habit is like giving up a worn pair
of slippers. It is much easier to do when there is a new
and better pair at hand. When the only apparent alterna-
tive is going barefoot, most people will hang on to their old
pair. The key to successfully quitting enabling, after one has
made a commitment to do so, is to exchange enabling for a
style of living that is warmer and more fulfilling.

Within the dynamics of enabler-dependent relationships, it is enablers who need to start changing first. If
enablers wait for their dependents to take the first step,
they may be waiting forever. Despite the illusion of having
near control over the dependent, the fact is that you don't
have control over anyone but yourself. If an enabler wants
to change, the enabler must initiate it.

As an enabler, you must begin by altering the structure
of your enabling relationships. Reassess all of the obligations
and duties you have assumed as part of your relationships
and return any of those obligations and duties which are
not yours to their rightful owners. Keep only those that
are legitimately yours. Since you will no longer have to
mind everyone else's business, you will have much more
time and energy for yourself. Without the excuse of "too
many responsibilities to others," you will be free to develop
talents that you have neglected.

Take time to really look at yourself. Make an inventory
of all of the interests and talents that are uniquely yours.
Once you have determined which among your interests
you want to develop, launch a program of activity. You can
be selfish about your choices because, in the long run, each
individual's self-development works for the good of all.

Whatever you decide to do doesn't have to consume
great amounts of time, but it does have to be your first

priority. Don't let any family member pressure you into giving up your plan. Your new life must come first. If it is only dinner with a group of friends on Thursday evening, and an exercise class on Friday morning, let nothing interfere. Start small, but start somewhere. Begin to create an identity for yourself, and then hang on.

As a reforming enabler, don't allow yourself to be intimidated or made to feel guilty about your projects. It is possible that when you begin to spend more time on yourself and less on your dependents, your dependents will escalate their demands and exaggerate the inconvenience your neglect is causing. Dependents are accustomed to being catered to and may try to maintain their position by sabotaging any plan or project you might start.

Developing friends outside of the family will also help you to establish an individual identity. These friends will not only feed your personal growth, but also give you the comfort of knowing that you have outside support to draw on should a relationship collapse. Friends soften the fears.

As your outside activities and interests grow, so will your self-esteem. It is essential to feel secure in your belief that what you are doing is best for everyone, and turn a deaf ear to complaints.

Beginning a new life based on realistic expectations and actual possibilities can look like an overwhelming undertaking, but it doesn't have to be. Slight changes in attitude and behavior make big differences. Anyone who chooses to take the necessary steps to stop enabling others will find a happier and more fulfilled life.

Altering yourself begins with:

1. Recognizing your enabling behavior.

2. Understanding the source of your enabling.

3. Making a commitment to change.

4. Facing the fear brought by change.

5. Accepting nothing but honesty from yourself and others.

6. Learning how to respond appropriately to the needs of others.

7. Developing your personal identity based on your unique talents and interests.

To keep yourself from enabling:

» Treat yourself no worse than you would treat anyone else.

» Learn to accept and forget about the things you can't change.

» Prioritize the things about yourself that you want to change. Start with whatever you decide needs attention first.

» Make decisions based on long-range goals instead of the short-term remedy, and act accordingly.

» Break your routine patterns. Changing routine can alter a situation.

» Cultivate the appearance of well-being and happiness. Take care of your clothes, your hair, your diet, and get exercise. Take loving care of yourself physically, mentally, and spiritually.

» Make friends of your own. Don't rely on your partner's or family's friends. Join clubs, become a volunteer, take classes, get a part-time job—whatever it takes to develop friends apart from your family or the dependent situation.

» Don't do anything for other people, including children, if they can and should be doing it for themselves.

» Demand that everyone in your family contribute their fair share of work.

16

INTERDEPENDENT LOVE

Certainly there are times when others close to you genuinely need help, care, and support. This makes it especially important to understand the distinction between help that makes others stronger and help that fosters their dependency. There is a difference between legitimate caring and enabling. Children do get hurt, husbands do need encouraging, wives do need support, and friends do need a listening ear. Everyone needs help at times, and it is important to be available to others when you are needed.

Enablers must find that line between healthy interdependence and destructive enabling-dependence—then help only when it is appropriate. Assessing a situation before jumping into the middle of it helps enablers respond in ways that discourage dependency. You should try to help when the need is genuine, but you should not rush in when your help will prevent others from learning the things they need to know—because that is not help.

The particular configuration of my husband's and son's conditions taught me that each person's path is unique. All of the challenges and troubles they were encountering were giving them the information they needed to walk down their path. The help I gave only served to block their way. By trying to remove obstacles for them, I stood in the way of them developing a life that worked for them. Leaving others to work toward their own rewards gives them the joy and self-esteem that comes from growth and mastery.

Now when I am confronted with a problem that is not mine, I tell myself not to interfere, that the problem needs to be solved by its owner. Since I started allowing others to tackle their own problems, I have been surprised by how ingenious and resilient they are.

When partners, children, parents, or friends have problems that are permanent, such as physical handicaps, it is even more important to allow them to come to terms with their situation as soon as possible, so that their chances of living life more fully are enhanced.

Enablers can begin altering the structure of their enabler-dependent relationships by reassessing their obligations and duties within those relationships. Then they should return all those obligations and duties, which they have taken over, to their rightful owners, keeping only the ones that are legitimately their own. Their challenge is to quit carrying everyone else and begin walking beside them.

Breaking the enabling game is a real test of love—and love, like charity, begins at home. I am not referring to the home of the hearth, but the home of the heart. The love you have for others is directly proportional to the love you have for yourself. It is because your capacity to love is based on the quality of your self-love that the pivotal point for helping those you love is taking care of yourself, providing for your own growth, and developing your own talents.

❦

Knowing and believing that there are things that you can do to change should bring you hope of new possibilities. And accepting that there are specific things about yourself and your life circumstances that can't be changed should give you the permission to quit struggling against them.

You don't have to be perfect, or a superhero. It is your very fallibility that leaves you with directions to grow. What would there be to learn if you already knew everything? How can anyone improve on perfection? If you are an enabler, you need to get off everyone else's case and get on your own.

NOTES

1. Cole, Diane, "Which Kids Succeed? Some Surprising News," *Family Weekly*, April 11, 1982, p. 7.

2. Meer, Jeff, "Mental Alertness and the Good Old Days," *Psychology Today*, March 1985, p. 5.

3. Stark, Elizabeth, "Tell It From the Mountain," *Psychology Today*, October 1985, p. 11.

4. Vandershaf, Sarah, "A Happy Pace," *Psychology Today*, January 1987, p. 68.

5. Meer, "Mental Alertness and the Good Old Days," p. 71.

6. Wood, Clive, "Their Own Worst Enemy," *Psychology Today*, February 1987, p. 18.

BIBLIOGRAPHY

Al-Anon. *Twelve Steps and Twelve Traditions.* New York: Al-Anon Family Group Headquarters, Inc., 1987.

Bandler, Richard, and John Grinder. *Reframing.* Moab, UT: Real People Press, 1982.

Beattie, Melody. *Codependent No More: Stop controlling Others and Start Caring for Yourself.* Center City, Minnesota: Hazelden Publishing and Educational Services, 2001.

Berger, John. *Ways of Seeing.* London: British Broadcasting Corp. and Penguin Books Limited, 1981.

Bower, Sharon Anthony, and Gordon H. Bower. *Asserting Yourself: A Practical Guide for Positive Change.* Cambridge, Minnesota: Da Capo Press, 2004.

Branden, Nathaniel. *The Six Pillars of Self-Esteem.* New York: Bantam, 1994.

Freeman, Arthur. *Clinical Applications of Cognitive Therapy.* Norwell, Minnesota: Kluwer Academic Publisher, 2004.

Friday, Nancy. *My Mother, Myself.* New York: Dell Publishing Co., Inc., 1979.

Glasser, William. *Choice Theory: A New Psychology of Personal Freedom.* New York: Harper Collins, 1999.

Harris, Thomas. *I'm OK—You're OK.* New York: Harper Collins, 2004.

Jourard , Sidney M. *The Transparent Self.* New York: D. Van Nostrand Co., 1971.

Maslow, Abraham. *Toward a Psychology of Being.* New York: Wiley and Sons, 1999.

Meer, Jeff. "And the Depressed Feel Better," *Psychology Today* (July 1985).

Schaef, Anne Wilson. *Co-Dependence: Misunderstood—Mistreated.* New York: W.H. Freeman and Co., 1992.

Seligman, Martin E. P. *Learned Optimism.* Pocket Books, 1998.

Watzlawick, Paul, John Weakland, and Richard Fisch. *Change: Principles of Problem Formation and Problem Resolution.* New York: W. W. Norton & Co. Inc., 1984.

Woititz, Janet Geringer. *Adult Children of Alcoholics.* Deerfield Beach, FL: Health Communications, Inc. 1990.

LaVergne, TN USA
28 January 2010
171542LV00001B/236/P